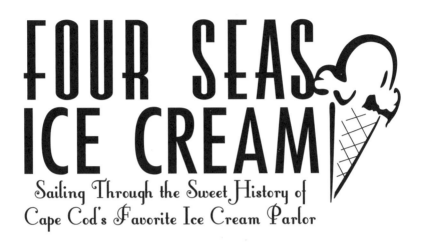

FOUR SEAS
ICE CREAM

Sailing Through the Sweet History of
Cape Cod's Favorite Ice Cream Parlor

D1564617

Heather M. Wysocki

Charleston | London

THE
History
PRESS

Published by The History Press
Charleston, SC 29403
www.historypress.net

Copyright © 2012 by Heather M. Wysocki
All rights reserved

Cover images: upper left, *painting by Joan Scudder*; bottom right, line outside store, *Studio by the Sea*; middle left, dripping cone, *Roots Workshop. All other photos from the Warren family collection.*

First published 2012

Manufactured in the United States

ISBN 978.1.60949.528.2

Library of Congress CIP data applied for.

CONTENTS

FOREWORD

Four Seas is special to so many people, and we are so excited about this book for several reasons. Personal involvement with the business and the author means that our stories are told in a way some of Four Seas' fans might never have heard before. Plus, we've always wanted to document our story and share it with our friends, alumni, family and fans.

After my father, Dick Warren, wrote *The Complete Idiot's Guide to Homemade Ice Cream* in 2006, we were hoping that he would do a book on just Four Seas Ice Cream and its long history in Centerville and with our family. However, between publicity for the recipe book and spending time doing his favorite things—golfing, skiing and being with his family—time slipped away, and my dad died in 2008 in a skiing accident. A few years after his passing, in 2011, we were approached to do this project. Lucky for us, we have an amazing and award-winning writer, our daughter, Heather Wysocki. She spent countless hours researching, interviewing, writing and combing through photos, newspapers, magazines, awards, books and memorabilia for this complete history of Four Seas Ice Cream. Heather has also worked many years at the store, helps write newsletters for Four Seas and has worked several years writing for local newspapers. I often joke that she was a better writer at four years old than I am now.

Four Seas has been in our family for over fifty years now. I'm a second-generation owner. My parents, Richard and Georgia, met while working at Four Seas in the 1950s and ran the place for twenty years. My father continued running the store and, in the 1980s, married Linda. Everyone in the family has worked at the store, from my sister Janice to my late brother Randy. In fact, you could say that as soon as you could reach the counter while standing on a milk crate you were put to work, labeling quarts and pints or helping wash up. Even before that, we were fixtures at the store. My siblings and I have all been told that when our mom was working at the store, we would visit with customers from our playpens. Even though she's a new addition to the family, my wife, Peggy, has completely immersed herself in our crazy and rewarding business, spending long hours at the store and behind the scenes, living on a few hours of sleep every night. We have worked countless hours dishwashing, scrubbing, scooping, painting, making ice cream, doing freezer work, making friends with customers and co-workers and making smiles.

The family tradition continues today. My son Joshua still is one of our managers and ice cream makers, while our daughter Heather worked at the store as a scooper and manager for nine years. My nieces Lindsey, Paige and Eliza have spent summers on Cape Cod and always help behind the counter. My stepsister worked at the store as a teenager and still helps us out at the end of the summer, and my stepbrother, who lives in New Hampshire, also comes down when he can. And Linda gets in on the action too, helping us make sandwiches and keeping the store running smoothly at the beginning and end of each summer when many of our regular employees are in school or away at college. From our decades in the business, we have a unique insiders' perspective on Four Seas that we're really excited to share with you.

It is amazing to us how many people the store affects, from the customers to the crew. Over the years, we have heard many touching stories and memories tied to the store, and we love hearing them all. It seems like everyone has a joyful experience from Four Seas that they continue to hold in their memories.

In this ever-changing world, it is so fun to be part of a business that is historic, unchanged and creates memories and smiles. We were hoping "Chief" was going to do this project, but we are proud that Heather was able to write this and share our family business and story with everyone. Hopefully, this book and the store will build memories and bring smiles for a long time to come.

Douglas and Peggy Warren
Owners, Four Seas Ice Cream

INTRODUCTION

G elato. Sorbetto. Sprinkles and candies and crumbles.

Four Seas does not do these things. Four Seas does not make trendy flavors or follow the low-fat craze. There are no sprinkles on the ice cream cones, no cookies in the ice cream sundaes, no lettuce or tomato on the fresh lobster salad sandwiches. But for over seventy-seven years, thousands of families and visitors to the seaside Cape Cod town of Centerville have flocked to the store and stood in line for hours for exactly that simplicity.

A quarter-mile from Craigville Beach, Four Seas Ice Cream is situated in a quaint village of postcard dreams, complete with the white church where generations have married and the next-door candy shop where generations of those couples' children have purchased sweets.

Over the years, Four Seas has become the siren's call for visiting families and some very famous neighbors: the Kennedys, whose love of Four Seas Ice Cream has been documented in local and national newspapers.

But despite national recognition by the media and its stars, Four Seas came from a humble place. In 1934, a Boston insurance man teamed up with a restaurateur friend to transform an old blacksmith's shop into a seasonal seaside ice cream shop. Within just a few years, the business was bleeding money. But owner W. Wells Watson was a New Englander, and the Yankee sensibility of bucking up and doing what needs to be done came through.

After he officially took over from the restaurateur, the business became more successful than any seven-table ice cream shop has the right to be. And it has stayed that way.

In 1960, Richard Warren, a just-out-of-college teacher who worked at the shop in the summers, purchased the business with his wife, Georgia, whom he met when she was behind the counter at Four Seas during her family's summer trips to the Cape. Over the years, the Warren family faced tragedy and divorce but ultimately transformation with the second marriage of Warren to Linda Joyal in 1984, to whom he was married until his death in 2008. In 1999, another change came when Richard and Linda Warren began transitioning ownership of the business to Richard's son Douglas and his new wife Peggy, who still run the store. Until 2010, the store didn't even open in winters, despite requests from fans of the ice cream.

Through all these changes, one thing has stayed pretty much the same: Four Seas. While fresh coats of paint have been added and new employees have scooped, the ice cream and the feeling customers have when they bite into a cone hasn't changed—and never will. Ask anyone associated with Four Seas—from customers to neighbors to the former employees whose children now yearn to work there—and you'll hear a story of old-fashioned family values, a commitment to quality and a deep love of community.

There are no pints with the owners' faces on them, no national franchises and no complicated dishes. But there are ice cream cones, smiling children with sandy toes and decades of knowledge about good ice cream, good service and good summers by the sea.

It may be old-fashioned, but that's the way the people who love Four Seas like it.

Chapter 1

WE FACE FOUR SEAS

How the Store Came to Be

Like the name of the store itself, the village of Centerville, in the town of Barnstable and where Four Seas is located, got its inspiration from the sea. Centerville started as Chequaquet and was settled as early as 1669. However, it didn't gain a true population of full-time residents until the 1800s, as the Atlantic Ocean peninsula of Cape Cod came into focus as one of the nation's greatest fishing regions. Though many of the larger vessels sailed instead from Boston; Hartford, Connecticut; and the off-Cape islands of Nantucket and Martha's Vineyard, the small village of Centerville dipped its toe in the waters of seafaring as well.

From 1820 to 1860, the Crosby family ran a shipbuilding company before family members eventually moved their shop. Their legacy still exists; the Crosby Boat Yard is still in operation. The stately home of one of those seafarers, Captain Mazeppa Nickerson, sits nearby, and the mid-nineteenth-century James Crosby House, originally a stagecoach stop, still houses Centerville residents.

Across the street, Fernbrook, a Queen Anne–style mansion, boasts acres of rolling hills and ponds, the setting for many a courtship and hundreds of weddings. Its grounds were designed by Frederick Law Olmsted, renowned for his design of New York City's Central Park. Owned first by Herbert Kalmus, the inventor of Technicolor, the huge home-turned-inn hosted the likes of Walt Disney and Richard Nixon.

Despite a rather lukewarm view of the Revolutionary War from the town of Barnstable as a whole, several early Centerville residents fought in it. By

An aerial view of the village of Centerville, the quaint seaside village where Four Seas is located. Many of the same old sea captains' homes still stand. *Courtesy of Nickerson Archives.*

the dawn of the Civil War, the village and its residents were taking a much more proactive approach. One man who owned a home on Centerville's Main Street, Russell Marston of Marstons Restaurants in Boston, was an outspoken abolitionist who seemed to goad others into the same stance.

In 1850, Centerville's denizens created a committee of three to draw up a document outlining the community's feelings against slavery. Not surprisingly for a northern location, the document was greeted with support by most residents. When the call came for volunteers to fight in the war, nineteen Centerville residents—a fairly large number of able-bodied men, at that time, to leave a community reliant on them for agriculture and fishing—answered. In comparison with some towns whose populations were decimated, town records report that only six men didn't return from the war.

The name Centerville was granted to the village in 1834 when it got its first post office. Around that same time, shops and a proper village center sprang up. In fact, Four Seas was not the first ice cream shop to open in Centerville.

In 1874, the Hallet family turned their confectionary store into an ice cream parlor. The building still stands and operates as the 1856 Country Store, selling sweets and gifts. Other old-fashioned enterprises were also centered in Centerville, including a saltworks that transformed the nearby seawater into useable salt; a mill; and cranberry bogs, some of which still produce the tangy fruits today.

Close enough to the ocean for the salt spray to weather its signature cottages and give generations of children a place to spend their summer days, Centerville is still a quaint village of just a few thousand people. Bolstered by the wealthy, equally historic village of Osterville and the Cape's commercial and residential hub, Hyannis, Centerville is the peaceful buffer between the Cape's two populations and has been a home for both its wealthiest and humblest residents. Its residents, both those who stay for the summers before returning to their off-Cape homes in the winters and those who weather the often bone-chilling winters, make their homes in those weathered cottages, just steps from the Centerville River, where children still jump off bridges before being chased off by older local residents.

Larger, multistoried homes still feature the so-called widows' walks where, hundreds of years ago, the heartbroken wives of sea captains waited for men who were never coming home. Shingles, conservative colors and lush, ancient trees characterize the village as a place with sentimental values not necessarily looking for a sprucing up (save during the annual Old Home Week event, when even the simplest homes get special treatment).

An early 1900s image of Craigville Beach, just one-quarter of a mile away from Four Seas Ice Cream and the place where generations of Four Seas family members have learned to swim. *Courtesy of Nickerson Archives.*

The South Congregational Church still stands on the corner, tolling its hourly reminder, and post–Sunday school, its young parishioners still stream into the next-door 1856 Country Store with its old-fashioned and welcoming benches outside. Around the corner on South Main Street, the Our Lady of Victory Church sits on land donated long ago by Kalmus, an amiable neighbor to the white-shingled congregational church on Main Street.

For generations, families' days revolved around religion and attending one of those two establishments—and they frowned on those who didn't feel the same. In 1846, a South Main Street resident was taken to task by village leaders for sharing liberal ideas with worshipers at the churches. His protests actually led village leaders to create a village hall for discussion, called first the Liberty Hall and later Howard Hall.

Down the road at Craigville Beach, a Christian camp and a tabernacle were built in 1871. The Christian Camp Meeting Association still attracts thinkers and worshipers every summer. But Centerville wasn't all innocence in the first decades of the twentieth century. Though the main village now lacks a proper restaurant or bar, in the 1920s another home, built by family of the owners of Fernbrook, served as a speakeasy.

As the Christian beach camp was gaining notoriety, Cape Cod itself was gaining a reputation as a summer resort. In 1875, the first cottages meant specifically for summer renters were built on a Centerville lake that hosted a charter fishing company. In the 1890s and early 1900s, development of the area continued to attract summer visitors whose professions kept them away during the winter, and the area grew into a tourist mecca. The social register *Who's Who on Cape Cod* listed the summer addresses of residents from as close as Boston and Providence, Rhode Island, to as far away as Detroit and St. Louis, Missouri. Wealthy industrialists, it seemed, relished the clean air and quiet roads after spending winters in the grittier cities in which they made their fortunes.

But even into the early twentieth century, and despite an influx of city-grown "summer people," Centerville kept its quieter way of life. From Craigville Beach, a winding road meanders through the village, past the tiny cottages and over the hill, where a greenhouse still produces local vegetables and flowers. Until just a few years ago, the one traffic light at South Main Street and Craigville Beach Road marked the only nod to transportation modernity in the quaint village.

Though just a mile away parts of Centerville have been transformed into an area of chain coffee shops, gas stations and shopping centers, the original "Centerville Four Corners" area still features just a handful of shops surrounded by those original cottages and captains' homes.

One travel writer, penning a humorous column for the 1936 *Cape Cod Handbook* under the name "The Grouch," wrote sarcastically about the area's "drawbacks":

> *I never bathe except in a bathtub and so the warm water bathing on sandy beaches does not appeal to me in the least. I do not like Cape Cod air as it is too sweet and soothing. I want the harsher air that makes one feel like getting up and doing something every minute. I do not like the little white Cape Cod cottages with roses running all over them…and I care nothing about early American history.*

Centerville Gets a Bit Sweeter

Centerville and its reputation for being the perfect summer respite from the hustle-and-bustle of Boston, New York City and other Northeast cities was what drew Four Seas Ice Cream's first owner to the area. At the time, the landscape of South Main Street was very different. A full-service restaurant called the Ye Olde Cape Codder was across the street before it, too, transformed, into a high-end clothing store called The Wool Shop. Across the street was Fuller's Market, which served as the village's go-to grocery store. And next door was the building that would become Four Seas, a one-hundred-year-old blacksmith shop that had until recently still been in operation.

"It was where the blacksmith did his shoeing for the horses. You can still see the runner where the barn door used to be at the entrance to Four Seas," Four Seas owner Douglas Warren says. The brother of the Ye Old Cape Codder restaurant's owner was a friend of W. Wells Watson—full name William Wells Wilberforth Watson—a Boston insurance salesman who reluctantly agreed to financially back the ice cream store. In a 1968 letter to Richard Warren, the father of Douglas Warren who operated Four Seas for nearly fifty years, Watson recalled the situation: "This brother, named Irving Wolff, was to operate the business and prove to me it would be a money-maker during the summer months only. I was only financially interested, putting up the entire amount of cash necessary."

The Four Seas property was rented from the Bacon family, who had purchased it decades earlier for $250. The land was put into Watson's name

Before becoming Four Seas Ice Cream, 360 South Main Street in Centerville was home to a blacksmith's shop run by T. Kelly Jr. of Centerville. His shop moved down the road in 1912, and a new building was built shortly after. *Courtesy of the Warren family.*

on the town records in 1935, and he would purchase the property in 1938 from the family for $6,500.

Before opening, the Four Seas property underwent major changes. The blacksmith shop, originally at the back of the property, was moved closer to the road and transformed into an area for freezer cabinets, from which employees would scoop and sell ice cream cones. There was no seating counter, no fountain for mixing up sodas and no sundaes. A freezer was located at the front of the building, and a passageway between the scooping area and the seating area was built. For decades, that area operated as a restaurant serving breakfast. In the afternoons and evenings, Four Seas Ice Cream patrons would enjoy treats there as well. A second part of the blacksmith shop building was moved just a few miles down the road to Osterville and still operates as a real estate agency.

The store was named after a poem, "Cape Cod Calls," by Mabel E. Phinney, which espoused appreciation for the four bodies of water surrounding Cape Cod: Cape Cod Bay, Buzzards Bay, the Atlantic Ocean and the Nantucket Sound.

An employee in the first few years at Four Seas. *Courtesy of the Warren family.*

Four Seas in its early years under W. Wells Watson. Watson would frequently run out of flavors because he only made a few gallons at a time. *Courtesy of the Warren family.*

"We face Four Seas," our slogan runs
Four Seas of azure blue.
And o'er them forth to foreign climes
have sailed good men and true
Our marshes lie in velvet browns,
Soft shades of russet tan,
And o'er them wheel the white winged gulls
A lone crow in the van.
Our beaches white with high piled dunes,
Where the Dusty Miller clings,
Are foils for the gay clad bather folk
Each recurrent season brings.
We're just a summer playground now,
Our glories in the past
"Cape Cod Calls" in joyous tones
Long made her prestige last.

A yellowing postcard featuring the poem is still kept in a frame by the door at Four Seas so curious customers can learn the origin of the name.

Despite Wolff's insistence that Four Seas, located smack-dab between the burgeoning tourist area of Centerville and the popular beaches of Craigville, would be a hit, Watson initially didn't see a return on his investment. He recalled in his 1968 letter that he "came back to Boston after the second year with a loss of over $600.00; I decided to take over the third year and prove it one way or the other. If non-profitable, I intended selling the equipment and moving out. Being in the insurance business, this was not difficult, as that business is normally quiet in summer due to vacations."

Quickly, Watson began seeing a profit, and the word about Four Seas started to spread. In just a few years, the business started to become profitable, and Watson began modernizing the nineteenth-century building. But just as he set about expanding the business, a hurricane hit Cape Cod in 1938, bringing many businesses to their knees. It could have spelled the end of Watson's quest to make Four Seas profitable, but luckily, the storm took out only a few trees and a neon sign hanging outside the store. The store has survived a half dozen hurricanes since.

A soda fountain with a counter and stools were added, and an engine room to fuel the freezers was built under the building. Due to the burgeoning summer business, Watson found himself nearly every year adding freezers and ice cream cabinets for scooping cones for hungry customers. Those

Four Seas Ice Cream original owner W. Wells Watson and his wife, Flo, in front of the ice cream store, 1956. *Courtesy of the Warren family.*

freezers, cabinets and soda fountain are still in existence today, with much of the same equipment being used. Watson's white-and-blue color scheme is also still seen in the floors, chairs and signature awnings at Four Seas.

His influence on some of the most popular flavors of Four Seas Ice Cream is also still seen, such as in the store's chip chocolate—not chocolate chip—and the flavor influenced by a traditional New England recipe for fudge called penuche.

In the early 1940s, Four Seas got its first jolt of fame when a Canadian radio commentator spent some time in Centerville and then went back to her home in Toronto to produce a five-minute radio broadcast entirely devoted to Four Seas. "She said she hoped the architecture, style and design of the building would never change, as it was also used as a meeting place for community friends," Watson wrote in his letter in 1968. An

Original owner W. Wells Watson in front of the "Four Seas Dairy Bar." *Courtesy of the Warren family.*

article in the local daily newspaper, then called the *Cape Cod Standard Times*, about the broadcast, "added tremendously and was a very cheap piece of advertising in those early days."

Much of Four Seas' continued success had to do with Watson's ability to pinch pennies in every aspect of his business, Douglas Warren says. "He was a stickler, he was a penny pincher. He went through the Great Depression and carried that into his business," Warren said.

With only a small amount of freezer space, Watson didn't believe in making enough ice cream for there to be any left at the end of the day. Instead, he made extremely small batches, just enough to get through the day, and simply told customers what he was out of as the stock dwindled throughout the day. Some days, when the seaside breeze wasn't enough to quell the heat and customers were desperate for a cool-down, the ice cream would be gone in a matter of hours. "He would open the store at noon and it would be gone by four o'clock," Warren says.

The breakfast menu served out of the sit-down area of Four Seas was handled separately by various people who rented the space, with breakfasts named after areas of the Cape such as "The Craigville Beach" special, Warren said. Until it was closed in 1959, the breakfast store provided a bit of additional income to Watson in the form of rent. But because breakfast was served only in the mornings, Four Seas Ice Cream began serving sandwiches during the lunch hours. Varieties of sliced meats and cheeses, old-fashioned delicacies such as cream cheese mixed with green olives or with dates and walnuts and seaside specialties such as lobster salad and crab salad were served. But Watson didn't have an employee make them, Doug Warren remembered. "He would have the neighborhood ladies make sandwiches in their homes and bring them up to Four Seas. When he had a lunch order, he would call one of the women with his order, like three tuna sandwiches. Then they would just run up the street to bring him the sandwiches."

It wasn't until the late 1950s that a kitchen was added to the back of the dining area. Then, employees—or, often, Doug's mother, Georgia—could make the sandwiches that would become nearly as synonymous with Four Seas as the ice cream, Doug Warren said. Eventually, the sandwiches became so popular that a sign advertising the store's "light lunches" was added.

His frugality and ingenuity—and ability to lean on the neighbors in his close-knit community—served Watson well as World War II rolled around. Across the country, families were losing loved ones in the war and feeling the pinch of shortages of goods that had once been plentiful. Victory

One of the first advertisements Four Seas Ice Cream ever put in the newspaper, including for the now-defunct breakfast shop. *Courtesy of the* Barnstable Patriot.

gardens cropped up, and families were urged to give up things like meat, chocolate and nylon stockings so that soldiers fighting overseas wouldn't have to go without.

Americans were also asked to give up sugar, leading to the rationing that severely challenged Watson in his quest to create homemade, from-scratch ice cream. And ice cream had been declared an essential food, meaning most Centerville residents were still clamoring to get it on a regular basis, Warren said. "Americans needed it for morale," he said. "So Watson started trying to scavenge it any way he could."

That led the ice cream maker to look in creative places for his goods. Watson wrote in his letter:

> *Due to rationing, it was difficult getting through the war years. A crowd each day was awaiting the opening at noon, and as desserts of all kinds were scarce, the supply of ice cream was sold out in three to three-and-one-half hours every day. Of course, gasoline was scarce, but ice cream was declared an essential food, so those who had gas could use it for the purchase of ice cream.*

To save his customers gasoline, which was also rationed, Watson would meet certain very loyal customers in Osterville, especially the Wianno and Oyster Harbors areas, so they wouldn't have to drive all the way to Four Seas. Every Sunday, groups of neighbors would come to "a certain corner" to trade for the ice cream, Watson said. "They later proved to be our heaviest users of our product, a very fine people, and very fine customers."

From 1934 until 1956, Watson worked every summer at the store and raised his family—children Barbara and Bill—with wife Florence, known often as Flo. Over the decades, the store's reputation grew with the help of Watson's dedication. He remembered in his 1968 letter:

> *By working sixteen hours a day, seven days a week, spoon sampling from the freezer room while it was in front, and friendly contact with people in the surrounding areas, the business eventually grew and became quite famous, with people coming from all over Cape Cod. And many from off the Cape knew of us through word of mouth, and often while they were on trips or visits they dropped in for some of our product.*

Employees, too, remember Watson as a dedicated store owner who was on shift most hours of the day. Though some evenings he would go home for dinner before returning for a few hours for the evening's post-dinner rush, often Watson would stay at the store for his supper as well. "Every day at 5:30 it was my job to heat up a TV dinner for Mr. Watson and serve it to him," former employee Saunie Chase Canuso said.

Dressed in his uniform of white pants and a white shirt, Watson was an unmistakable figure at Four Seas—even when that combination was covered in various colors of stains from the near-daily ice cream making he and the employees engaged in during Watson's ownership. Watson's ice cream maker could churn out

Four Seas original owner W. Wells Watson's daughter Barbara, age five, enjoying a Four Seas Ice Cream cone, 1937. *Courtesy of the Warren family.*

only about twenty gallons per day, meaning the sweet stuff had to be made on a daily basis to keep up with customers, current Four Seas Ice Cream owner Douglas Warren said.

The penny-pinching that Watson used to turn Four Seas into a successful business in its difficult first years and during World War II was on display every day. When he wasn't making ice cream, Watson spent much of his time visiting with customers and keeping an eagle-eye on employees. He often placed a chair so he could observe what went on behind the counter and would correct employees if the sizes of their ice cream cones were too big. At the time, an ice cream cone cost about fifteen cents, and Watson wasn't prepared to let even an additional cent's worth of ice cream go out the door. Favorite customers would often get a little extra on the cone or in a frappe from employees—but Watson watched so carefully that they were usually caught and gently reminded that the sizes of their cones were too large. For a favorite customer, Canuso said, "I would put about a half-pint of ice cream on that cone and every now and then Mr. Watson would catch me doing it."

Watson was known by customers and employees alike as an even-tempered, nice man who expected his employees to work extremely hard at whatever they were tasked with. Four Seas employees were expected to be clean-cut and respectful, no matter their age. Most employees began working at Four Seas the summer after their sophomore year in high school, when they were fifteen or sixteen years old. But Canuso was just thirteen years old when she approached Watson to work at the store. As one of six children, her mother decided she needed to get a job. "When he learned that I was thirteen, he asked me if I could 'be' fourteen. When I said I could, he gave me the job," Canuso said. But even though she was younger than the other employees, Canuso was expected to work just as hard, she remembered:

An employee making an ice cream soda, 1964.
Courtesy of the Warren family.

Mr. Watson was a very simple and nice man. There was nothing extravagant about him. And he was on site all the time. We all wanted to impress him with our work ethic…I don't remember ever having a day off. Our shifts were three days on, then three nights on, then three days on again and it went like that all summer long. But it was perfect. We had our days off to go to the beach and then when we worked the day shift, we had our evenings off.

Employees spent their long days doing everything from waiting on customers to making hot fudge to helping ice cream makers with the preparation work necessary to create ice cream on a daily basis. "We were on our feet the whole time, waiting on customers, washing dishes by hand, wiping down counters and tables and adding up the bill and doing the register," Canuso said. Though a male employee was designated as ice cream maker every year and would spend long days helping Watson make the ice cream, other employees were called into service when ice cream making became overwhelming. Employees would help prepare fruit for the fresh fruit ice cream flavors such as peach, cantaloupe and—at the time—blueberry, washing and peeling the fruit and turning it into purées. Employees would also help "mark packages," a Four Seas term that meant writing the name of the ice cream on every single quart or pint made. An employee would write the name of the ice cream on the bottom of every quart save vanilla. It was time-consuming but necessary to help employees know what flavors they were bringing to customers. Today, packages are still hand-marked, but now employees use pre-printed stickers to mark the flavor of every pint and quart.

Though on any given shift employees were busy doing everything from sweeping the floors to watering flowers or picking up trash in the parking lot, their main job, of course, was to serve ice cream to the lines of customers that visited. From the beginning, when Watson ran the business, the goal of Four Seas was to serve simple, high-quality ice cream and delicious toppings. Sundaes at the time of Watson's ownership were remarkably similar to those served at the store today. Like today, hot fudge was the most popular topping at the time. Out front in the scooping area, a machine kept hot fudge for sundaes hot, and employees would add two pumps of fudge to every sundae. A pot on a stove in a back room at the store was also kept warm at all times, and on very busy days, hot fudge was made seemingly constantly, Georgia Thomas remembered. Several types of chocolate were added to the fudge along with other ingredients, and it was every employee's duty to periodically stir the mixture so that it would melt evenly and not burn. Sundaes were served in paper cups that fit into larger metal cups to form sundae dishes. It allowed employees to throw out all dirty cups rather than wash every single one of them—a big help when there was no dishwasher for the hundreds of dishes that the store went through every day. Prices were much different at the time as well. A menu from the 1950s might have included prices such as twenty-five cents for a cone or just a few pennies for a glass of soda.

In the late 1940s and 1950s, business at Four Seas grew in leaps and bounds due to a combination of renewed spirit after World War II, a baby boom that brought in a lot of customers and their hungry children and the ability for most families to own a car to visit places like Four Seas that might not be down the street—especially those who were financially able to visit Cape Cod in the summertime. It was also the time when one of the most noticeable nods to Four Seas' popularity came into being. The store had always been busy, with customers waiting in the small counter area three or four deep for their ice cream. But in the 1950s, so many customers began

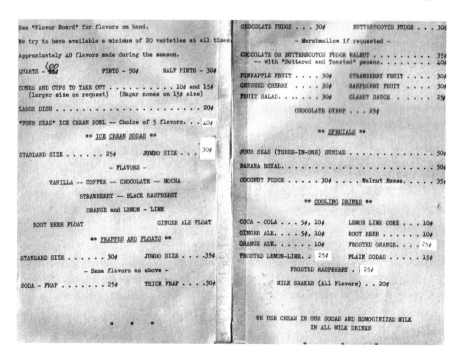

A Four Seas Ice Cream menu from 1952. *Courtesy of the Warren family.*

visiting Four Seas that the area wasn't large enough anymore, and lines began to form out the door—sometimes reaching dozens of feet into the parking lot. "Sometimes they'd line up all the way down the street. It was always busy, busy, busy but lots of fun. We got to know our regular customers, and we were always on the lookout for cute guys," Canuso said.

The busy days and nights paid off though. Watson started the Four Seas tradition of ensuring that his employees were shown appreciation for their hard work. At the end of every seventeen-week season, which ran from the week before Memorial Day to the week after Labor Day, Watson took his employees out for a gourmet dinner at a local restaurant to thank them for the summer. It's a tradition that continues at Four Seas to this day.

Around the time that Four Seas was becoming a Cape Cod landmark, Watson himself was beginning to think about retiring from running the shop that had been in his care for two decades. "I've always heard that he started thinking about selling the business in 1954," Douglas Warren said. Watson's two children, Barbara and Bill, had already expressed that they were not interested in taking over in order to keep the business in the family. By 1956, he had decided that he would retire at age sixty-five, just four short years away. In that time, he needed to find the right person to take over. Watson explained in his 1968 letter: "My plan was to screen students at Boston University until I found the exact type of person who I would want to continue the operation of the Four Seas in exactly the same manner as I had done for the past twenty-five years and not deteriorate the product in any way."

Chapter 2
FOUR SEAS IN THE EARLY WARREN YEARS

Watson's search went on for several months before a candidate emerged that he felt would be a good person to work at and eventually run his ice cream store. In the mid-1950s, a young man named Richard "Dick" Warren was attending Boston University with the goal of getting an education degree and becoming a teacher. He grew up on a farm in Saugus, Massachusetts, and in summers off from college, Warren would travel back home. For several years, he worked as a counselor at a summer camp for girls on the Maine coast to receive training for eventually becoming a teacher. But in the winter of 1956, Warren saw an advertisement on a bulletin board on the Boston University campus that caught his eye. A store called Four Seas Ice Cream was looking for a full-time manager and ice cream maker for the upcoming summer season. The job included a place to live, a big plus for a man who had never visited Cape Cod before and didn't have any connection to the area, let alone a family member's home he could stay in for the weeks the store was open between May and September. The apartment he was to be given was in the attic area of Four Seas and had been used by managers of the store so they were, literally, on site at all times. Though the area is now used as storage rather than as an apartment, it still goes by the name it acquired a long time ago in its former life as a residence: the Crow's Nest. "It sounded like a great opportunity to him, to come down here and work and live in the Crow's Nest," son Douglas Warren said.

The young college student didn't have too much experience with ice cream. As a toddler visiting his grandfather at his central Maine farm, little

Richard had helped crank up the sweet treat in a manual ice cream maker. And his mother would make ice cream about once a month on her old White Mountain brand crank freezer. He gained a small amount of experience while working for the girls' camp, when the chef would coax the four boys working as maintenance men into making ice cream every Sunday for the 225 hungry campers. But despite only two years of intermittent ice cream making, Warren was exactly what Watson was looking for, as he wrote in his 1968 letter about Four Seas: "After interviewing many, many young men, I found that Dick was the ideal type. It was his personality, hard work and love for the idea of Four Seas."

A young Warren traveled to Cape Cod for the first time in the spring of 1956 to become Watson's go-to manager and ice cream maker. Through his work making ice cream and as a manager of the store at night, Warren worked nearly constantly. Watson's idea was for whomever he picked as a manager that year to be the person he wanted to eventually take over the store. To that end, he offered partnership in the business during Warren's first year working there. Watson hoped that by the spring of 1960, Warren would be ready and willing to take over Four Seas permanently.

Unbeknownst to either Watson or Warren, working at Four Seas would not only provide a summer business while Warren taught in the winters; it also was the place where he would meet his future wife. In 1954, a young woman named Georgia Swift had just finished her sophomore year of high school in Braintree, Massachusetts, a town about an hour from Cape Cod, when she accepted a job at Four Seas to work behind the counter during summers. For decades, her family had owned several small homes on Lake Wequaquet, a large body of water in the village of Centerville. The Swift family spent every summer on Cape Cod enjoying sailing on Wequaquet Lake, events at its namesake yacht club and the other summer activities that attract thousands to Cape Cod and Centerville every year. "And we were there every weekend as long as the weather was nice," Georgia remembered. Her brother Joe also worked at the store in 1955 in the job still known as "morning boy," the person in charge of cleaning and stocking the shop for the day ahead. Working at Four Seas wasn't just work for Swift; she and the other employees became friends, she said. "I loved working there, and I loved the other kids I was working with. We did a lot together. We sailed, we'd go swimming after we got off work. That really developed some wonderful relationships with people who I'm still in touch with to this day."

In 1956, Swift had just graduated high school and would be heading off to Fisher Junior College in Boston in the fall. But as she had the previous two summers, she came to Centerville with her family for the summer and worked at Four Seas Ice Cream. It was the same year that Richard Warren accepted the managing job for the store.

Quickly, Georgia Swift, then eighteen years old, and Dick Warren, then twenty-one, began dating and spending time over the summer together and with other Four Seas employees. Luckily for the young couple, they would be attending college near each other. In the fall of 1956, Swift began her studies at Fisher Junior College, a two-year school in the town of Somerville, just outside Boston. The school offered classes in secretarial skills, accounting and bookkeeping, among other subjects. Swift studied accounting. Just a few miles away, Warren was heading back to Boston University for his senior year of college. The couple continued to date through the winter, "and we got more and more serious as time went by. In December he gave me his fraternity pin," Georgia Swift (now Thomas) said. That symbol of commitment led to plans for marriage, and in 1957, the couple was married at the white congregational church on Main Street in Centerville, just around the corner from Four Seas Ice Cream.

What followed were a few hectic years as the Warren family began to grow at the same time that Warren's career was taking off. Around the time of his wedding to Georgia Swift, Dick Warren took a job as a junior high school teacher in Westfield, Massachusetts, in the western part of the state. The following spring, the couple moved to Cape Cod after Dick Warren accepted a job teaching at Barnstable High School. The couple rented the first floor of a home in Hyannis that was eventually turned

A staff photo from 1962. New owner Richard "Chief" Warren is at left. *Courtesy of the Warren family.*

Four Seas Ice Cream in 1959, the year before owners Richard and Georgia Warren purchased the store from original owner W. Wells Watson. *Courtesy of the Warren family.*

into a gas station. In March of that same year, the couple's first child, daughter Janice, was born. They only lived in the rented home for a year before Georgia's grandfather passed away and the young couple's help was needed at her grandmother's home. The Chestnut Street property owned by Georgia's grandparents included a large home, where they lived, plus a smaller one, which the young couple moved into so Georgia could keep an eye on her grandmother. That summer, Watson finally approached the Warrens about taking over Four Seas Ice Cream and purchasing the business. "That summer, Mr. Watson talked to Dick about the business because he knew neither of his two children were going to be involved," Thomas said.

By 1959, the young couple had signed an agreement that they had a year to consider taking over the business and to have the right of first refusal to purchase it. Georgia was just twenty-three years old and Dick just three years older. So with a young daughter and a new home, the Warrens purchased Four Seas from Watson, borrowing money from Georgia's grandmother and a local bank to pay for it. In the winters, Dick Warren would teach at Barnstable High School, and he would run Four Seas in the summer. For a month at the beginning of the season and again at the end of the summer, school was still in session and he tried to juggle both a busy ice cream shop and teaching teens at the local school. Son Doug Warren said, "The school was great because it meant a steady income when Four Seas was closed, and he was able to afford a nicer home. He tried to sink every dime he made at Four Seas back into the business, so especially at first it was a very small salary. After he retired, he didn't know how he managed it, he said."

Over the next few years, the Warren family grew to include two more children. Randall, or Randy as he was known by family and friends, was born in 1961. Doug followed in 1963. Just six months after his birth, the couple moved their burgeoning family to a home on Hi-ona-Hill Road, literally just a few hundred feet down the road from Four Seas. The children added a new element to running the ice cream store, Georgia Thomas said. As a baby, Janice was placed in a playpen in the kitchen area while her mother prepared sandwiches for Four Seas customers. "At the time, we had sandwiches brought into the store in cellophane bags. So I didn't have to make the sandwiches, I just had to get them ready for the customers. And I had Janice in the playpen, which was sort of tough in a way. But it ended up working out fine, and the customers just loved that little baby in her playpen."

Randy and Doug also took their turns in the playpen while their mom helped at Four Seas, preparing sandwiches during the day and helping ensure the store ran smoothly. After Randy was born, a babysitter helped during the day as well. As the children got older, Georgia was able to do certain things for the store while at home or while the children were watched by a neighbor or babysitter. The store's homemade brownies, used in brownie ice cream sundaes and as a take-to-the-beach treat, were made in the Warrens' home oven so that Georgia could watch the children at the same time.

At the beginning and end of the summer season, when Dick Warren was busy teaching, the children would be put on the bus and Georgia would spend the school day working at Four Seas before meeting the children at

Along with ice cream, Four Seas serves classic seaside sandwiches, including lobster salad. The store sells a couple hundred lobster salad sandwiches every day in the summer. *Photo by the author.*

the bus stop around 2:30 p.m. every day. Before Four Seas opened its doors the weekend before Memorial Day for its seventeen-week season, the couple would make the ice cream that would be needed in the first few days. The first few weeks of every season, especially in the first few years the Warrens owned Four Seas, were difficult. The weather during spring on Cape Cod, like across the rest of New England, can vary from beautiful and warm—perfect ice cream weather—to pouring rain and near-freezing temperatures. On those less-than-nice days, customers were extremely scarce. "We might have taken in fifty or sixty dollars a day at that point in the season, because it was still so cold. But usually a few weeks in it would be busy," Georgia said.

As leader of the speech and debate club at the high school, Dick Warren was often away on trips with students or for training, and Georgia also became in charge of the day-to-day operation of the store, she said. "I wasn't there quite as often as Dick, but when he was gone on a trip I'd be there, and I would make ice cream with whoever the ice cream maker was at that point. I'd spend a lot of hours there. But that's how it works when you're trying to keep a business going, trying to make a profit. It was hectic, but hey—we were young, we were willing to work hard and that's what you do when you've got a business."

Owner Richard Warren makes ice cream with an employee, 1970s. *Courtesy of the Warren family.*

The Warrens quickly became synonymous with Four Seas because of their commitment to reaching out to their customers, both at the store and in the community. The couple made a point of getting to know their regular customers and asked about their lives at each visit. Likewise, cocktail parties and golf outings at the local Cummaquid Golf Club let them make friends from the village of Centerville and surrounding villages such as Osterville, Barnstable and Cummaquid.

In the first few years after the Warrens purchased Four Seas, the building itself underwent major changes in response to the growing popularity of the little Centerville ice cream store. One of Dick Warren's first moves was to replace W. Wells Watson's original, aging ice cream maker with one with a larger capacity. When Watson ran the store, the small-batch freezer still couldn't keep up with the customers' orders, and the store would sometimes run out of ice cream on busy weekend nights. To make sure that didn't happen, Warren bought a new ice cream freezer that doubled the store's output and ensured no customer had to go without his or her favorite flavor. At the time, only one small walk-in freezer was on the property to hold all of the store's ice cream—pints, quarts and tubs for scooping cones and sundaes. But for the same reason he purchased a new ice cream maker, Dick Warren also set about expanding Four Seas and increasing the space where ice cream could be stored. He added a small walk-in refrigerator to store sandwich fixings, nuts, candies and flavorings, and then added a second small freezer when the children were still young.

In the store's early years, its parking area looked very different from its current setup. There were just a handful of parking spots for customers, and on busy nights, cars were allowed to park across the street at a luxury clothing store that was only open during the day. A second parking area was leased from the fire department for one dollar per year because the department didn't use that piece of property. But a bid to build a fire station in the area led to a lengthy battle between Dick Warren and fire officials. Eventually, Warren was off the hook—the fire station was built up the street instead, and the parking area is still used by Four Seas. A third, larger parking area was also the subject of a battle between Warren and the owner of a hotel that moved in across the street. The two men both wanted to purchase a plot of land for parking because patrons of both establishments were in the habit of parking along South Main Street when the hotel or ice cream store's parking lots filled up. According to Warren family lore, the

A Four Seas Ice Cream advertisement from 1977. Four Seas, despite being busy since its early days in the 1930s, did not begin to advertise until the 1960s. *Courtesy of Nickerson Archives.*

hotelier's bid for the lot was accepted by its owner, a woman from New Jersey, first. But Dick Warren took advantage of the fact that no money had yet exchanged hands and drove to the woman's New Jersey home with cash in hand. She accepted, and Warren purchased the parking lot. "But we still let the hotel customers use the parking lot when their lot is full," Doug Warren said.

PART OF THE FOUR SEAS FAMILY

Though the combination of Dick's teaching salary and a small amount of income from Four Seas provided the young family with the ability to live a comfortable life, their lives as restaurateurs sometimes put a strain on other parts of their lives. As a child, Doug remembers that his parents were often difficult to see unless he visited Four Seas himself. Dick Warren was at the store from very early in the morning until late at night, unless the couple had a social engagement or a tee time. And Georgia was busy taking care of the couple's home and helping out at the store, especially at the beginning and end of every summer. Doug Warren said:

> *At an early age, sometimes it was up to me to make my own food. My mom tried to be around but it was nice in those days anyway because in the neighborhood everybody knew everybody else and we all took care of each other. A third of the older ladies who come into the store today say they babysat me when I was a little boy. I would swear I had over a thousand babysitters based on all the stories I hear now that I run the store.*

Much of young Doug's time was spent on his own or with other members of the close-knit Centerville neighborhood in which he lived. When his older siblings were working or unable to spend time with him, Doug would ride his bike to visit family still living on Lake Wequaquet or go to the beach with his neighborhood buddies. Fernbrook, the palatial Queen Anne mansion built in the early 1900s, was a particular source of fun. Its manicured grounds held one of Doug's favorite attractions as a child—a koi fishpond he visited on a regular basis, just down the street from the penny candy store. Visits to the koi pond, candy store or playground were often followed with—what else—a visit to Four Seas Ice Cream to see Dad and sneak a few spoonfuls of ice cream from under the watchful but lenient eyes of the teens working behind the counter, Doug Warren said. "It seemed like if I ever wanted to

Owner Richard Warren with current owner and son Douglas Warren at eighteen months old in the kitchen of Four Seas. *Courtesy of the Warren family.*

see my dad I had to come up here. Plus, I always wanted to get samples, so I'd hang out and hope someone would get me some ice cream, or I'd go into the cooler to steal a piece of cheese or a handful of nuts or candies. But apparently I was bratty, so the employees would sometimes lock me in the freezer as a joke."

Randy, the older of the two Warren sons, wasn't immune to retaliation from the older employees, either. When he first started working at the store, he, too, was locked in the freezer—as well as bombarded with trash as he came through doorways. "Oh, we used to pick on Randy all the time when he first started. He had freckles and bright red long hair and was kind of goofy looking. But he was hilarious," former Four Seas employee Dave LeMarbre said.

But there were perks that came with being the children of ice cream store owners, too. A major bonus that came along with being a member of the family was the once-a-year treat all the Warren children were allowed, and one they looked forward to all summer long, Doug said. Each child was allowed to have a banana split for dinner just once a year. The kids picked the date of their special dinner, but once they had it, they were back to regular dinners, with ice cream as an occasional treat.

It was in Randy and Doug's childhood years that Dick Warren gained the nickname by which generations of Four Seas employees and customers have known since, Doug Warren said:

In the first dozen or so years that he owned the store, people just knew him as Dick Warren or Mr. Warren, for the employees. But around 1970, Randy and I were in Indian Guides, and our dad came with us to our meetings. The group was sort of like Boy Scouts, but each person had an "Indian" name and created a totem pole to reflect it. At the meetings, we also wore paper headdresses with feathers in them. Well, one time my dad forgot to take his headband off after the Indian Guides meeting and ended up wearing it into Four Seas. One of the employees started calling him Chief, and it quickly became his nickname for the summer. And then after that it just stuck. Because he sort of was the chief of the place, the head honcho of Four Seas.

As the children grew older and required more than just the occasional hug or rattle shake while they sat in their playpens, Georgia began to do the store's bookkeeping from home as well in order to spend more time there. Because of her accounting background from Fisher Junior College, she was able to take over all the accounting and was eventually made treasurer and vice-president of Four Seas Ice Cream, Inc., the original corporation run by Dick Warren. Though Janice, who was a few years older than Randy

A classic Four Seas banana split—homemade vanilla, chocolate and strawberry ice creams with hot fudge, pineapple and strawberry toppings. *Photo by the author.*

and Doug, was already working at the store behind the counter, it didn't take long for the two boys to be roped into service at the family business as well. "The boys started working at the store at a very young age. They might have picked up the parking lot, or they might have done dishes or marked packages, little jobs like that," Georgia Thomas said. "They didn't start officially working at the store until they were in high school, like the other employees, but they were always around sweeping and doing things like that."

Sister Janice worked at the store for about five years before deciding to move on to another job at a diner in town. Though Janice's grades were up to snuff as far as Four Seas was concerned—Warren wouldn't hire anyone who didn't perform well in their classes at Barnstable High School—it was time for her to move on, Doug said. "She wanted to see if she could get a job on her own. She had the grades to get a job at Four Seas if she wasn't part of the family, but she also knew the job was hers because she was in the family." Doug and his brother Randy were a bit different, he said; their grades weren't quite as good as Warren would require for his employees, which meant they both tried to work even harder to prove themselves, Doug said.

> I knew I couldn't get this job any other way, but I knew I could work hard. I felt I had to prove myself. And that's the way Chief always was, too. He hustled, and you had to hustle. That's how he played tennis, that's how he played racquetball and that's how he ran his business. You might not be the best at what you're doing, but if you're the hardest worker, to him, that was sometimes even more important. My dad's phrase was that you had to be a "Johnny Hustle." You just give 110 percent.

Around age twelve, Doug began working at the store as "morning boy," a phrase used at Four Seas to describe what is known at most businesses as a janitorial or maintenance position. Each morning, Doug—and dozens of teens since—arrived early in the morning to scrub the floors, clean up any messes from the night before and restock what the ice cream scoopers would need the next day, from cones to toppings to gallons of ice cream. The job also required Doug to come in at night to help clean and do dishes. Five days a week, he came in from seven o'clock in the morning until around noon and then returned at seven o'clock in the evening and worked until around eleven, Doug said.

He stayed in the position for four years until being promoted to working behind the counter—the first time a male had held the position of server.

The Four Seas Ice Cream annual crew, with owner Richard "Chief" Warren (first row, far left), current owner and son Douglas (first row, third from right) and son Randy Warren, who died in 1983 (first row, far right). *Courtesy of the Warren family.*

Until the mid-1970s, Four Seas was staffed only by female servers. Men served as managers. *Courtesy of the Warren family.*

Previously, shifts were made up of four teenage girls and overseen by a male manager. The groups stayed together on the same shifts each summer, allowing the teens to get to know one another extremely well, Doug said. His entrée into working as the store's first male server didn't go as well as he'd hoped, he said—and customers sometimes had very strange reactions to seeing a boy behind the counter. "On the very first table I was assigned to wait on, a woman was just about to breast-feed her baby when I walked over. She expected a girl to wait on her table, because until that moment only girls had served tables. She was shocked and embarrassed by me coming up to the table—and so was I. That was my introduction to waiting on tables. And I still hate it."

While Doug was still too young to work as a manager or ice cream maker at the store, older brother Randy quickly began making a name for himself as one of Four Seas' stars. He worked at the store for nine summers, Doug for eleven. Like their father, Randy was very competitive and apt to make sure everyone knew he was the hardest worker in the store, Doug said. But like Chief and Georgia, he also seemed to charm customers and employees alike. "He always had a million people around him," Doug said.

From early on, it was clear that Randy, the oldest son, would be poised to take over Four Seas once his father eventually retired. Doug remembered:

> *Right from the get-go, Randy was going to take over the business. After just a few years, Jan went to find another job without Dad's help. And I wanted to be some sort of designer or architect. I was always drawing things. I always thought I wouldn't mind running the business, but Randy really wanted it. He just loved the business, and he always wanted to be there. He made it very clear from high school and into college that he wanted to take over the business. He even went into college for business, to make it clear that he would do whatever he needed to take over Four Seas.*

Many of the personality traits that made Dick Warren a successful proprietor of the busy store were also evident in Randy, Doug said. Randy was outgoing and loved pleasing customers, but his work ethic and drive to make Four Seas successful were echoes of his father's. "He was always smiling, always happy and didn't take things too seriously. Except for Four Seas. But he worked hard and was very competitive, whether it was playing sports or games with me or working."

The late Randall Mark Warren, son of Richard Warren and brother of Douglas Warren, for whom a Four Seas scholarship fund is named. *Courtesy of the Warren family.*

A TIME OF CHANGE

Over the next few years, as the Warren family's children grew older and the store grew busier, a tragedy and a divorce changed the trajectory of Four Seas forever. In 1981, when Doug was eighteen years old and just starting college, Dick and Georgia Warren separated. Janice and Randy were on their own at that point, having flown the nest several years before to raise a family and attend college, respectively. But the youngest son, Doug, had just recently entered college. The family doesn't talk much about what led to the separation, but Doug said that things had been tense between the couple for a few years when they agreed on a trial separation. "I saw some writing on the wall that it might possibly happen, as much as I didn't want it to happen. My mom waited until I was out of high school and then she wanted to split up and spend some time apart, see if it could fix things between the two of them."

But a happy ending wasn't in the cards. Just over two years later, the couple decided to officially divorce. Along with ending family life as the

Warrens had known it, Doug believes the split was also the end of the couple's consideration of opening a second location of Four Seas Ice Cream or expanding in any other way. The toughest part of the divorce for the Warrens' children was their battle over their assets, especially the business itself. Dick Warren balked at splitting the assets evenly, Doug said.

> *My mom was very much part of the store, and without her being there the store would never have happened. My dad was the front man of the store, but without her support it never would have happened. Allowing her to handle the children and the home and making sandwiches and handling the bookkeeping allowed him to focus on all the critical things he needed to focus on. My dad was never happy about splitting the business fifty-fifty. But she was absolutely deserving of half of everything, and it saddened me to see that he didn't really respect what she did for the business. I don't want to paint him in a bad light but I don't think he respected what she did for the business. It was very hard for us kids.*

After the divorce, Dick and Georgia went their separate ways, with Dick continuing to run the business. But the couple was thrown back together just months later. Just a few months before the couple's divorce became final, the Warrens were struck with tragedy. In March 1983, just a few weeks after he turned twenty-two years old, Randy Warren was hit and killed by a car while he was celebrating spring break in Fort Lauderdale, Florida. In an instant, one of the people whom customers most associated with the store was gone. Doug was twenty years old when his older brother, who was destined to take over the ice cream store, died. Away at school at the time of Randy's death, Doug had to take some time off from classes. That summer, the jovial atmosphere that Four Seas was known for was instead somewhat somber, as employees and customers alike remembered the smiling redhead who had worked at Four Seas for nine years and had played there as a child for years longer. "It was difficult to go to the store and hear condolences. I remember the hundreds of people who came out to say sorry. It was remarkable. But that summer is almost a blur to me. I guess I don't really remember that summer at the store because I don't want to remember the pain. I just want to remember all the great times," Doug said.

Between the divorce and the death of his oldest son and eventual business partner, Dick Warren underwent a transition, too, his other son said. Growing up, the family placed a lot of importance on attending Sunday church services at the Federated Church of Hyannis, just a few

41

miles away from Centerville in the most populated village on Cape Cod. When the children were young, Dick Warren even served as a deacon at the church. But after Randy's death, Dick Warren's commitment to church waned. "I think he started questioning why God would take his son. You never get the answers to those questions, though. After Randy's death, if I could pinpoint one thing that changed in my dad, it would be that he became less religious. After that, I only saw him at churches for weddings or funerals," Doug said.

At one point, it was a foregone conclusion that Randy would take over Four Seas Ice Cream when Dick chose to retire. But after his death, the question of who would take over came to the forefront of the family's mind once again but stayed unanswered for decades. "Keeping the business in the family was always one of my dad's big dreams. It wasn't overly discussed, but it was definitely brought up here and there. The problem was that he wanted me to go out into the world and carve my own niche first. Before Randy's death, he had always offered to help me if I ever wanted to open a second store—but eventually. He always believed that it was important for me to make my way in the world, though," Doug said.

To honor Randy, the family set up the Randall Mark Warren Memorial Scholarship Fund in 1983. Every year, the fund provides scholarships to deserving Four Seas Ice Cream employees and other Barnstable High School seniors who are heading off to college. Each year on a set-aside day at the beginning of the season, Randy's life is celebrated at the store with Randall Mark Warren Scholarship Day. On that day, 50 percent of Four Seas' proceeds are donated to the scholarship fund, and most employees choose to donate the tips they receive that day as well. Since its creation in 1983, the Randall Mark Warren Scholarship Fund has given out upward of $70,000 in college scholarships to employees and other students.

After the Warrens' divorce and the death of their son Randy, Dick Warren was just a little different than before, his son said. "I just don't think anybody's going to be the same person they were after losing a child," Doug said. But happier times were around the corner when Dick began dating a woman he met in 1982, after he and Georgia separated. Linda Joyal was a bookkeeper for Gunstock Mountain Resort in Gilford, New Hampshire, who was raising two teenage children alone. In her spare time, which wasn't much, Joyal enjoyed many of the same activities that Dick did—golfing in the spring and summer and skiing in the winter. It was during a golf outing in October 1982 that the two met—though sparks didn't exactly fly immediately.

"I was playing golf with a girlfriend at Pheasant Ridge Golf Club. We were on the first tee when a lady and gentleman asked to join us. We were fine with it. The gentleman kept coming up and talking to us, but I didn't think anything of it," Linda remembered. However, just a few months later, the man—Dick Warren—sought Linda out again, this time at the ski resort where she worked and where he had brought his family for years. Though it took some prodding, one of her employees eventually convinced her to talk to Dick. "But I thought that the woman he was golfing with in October was his wife, so I told him that I didn't date married men. And I didn't. But he said he wasn't married, so I said okay."

It may have sounded romantic but for one noticeable presence: Randy. "The entire time he's asking me out, there's this kid in the background with red hair and a ski hat just laughing hysterically," Linda said. The encounter was the only time that Linda would meet Randy, who died a little over a year later. After that first conversation, Linda and Dick got together periodically whenever he was able to head to New Hampshire and the two weren't busy—which wasn't often. Dick was still working at Barnstable High School, at this point as a teacher and guidance counselor, plus running Four Seas in the summer. Linda, too, worked a full-time job and was busy raising her children, Jennifer and Michael. "If he was busy, we didn't see each other, or if I was busy, we'd go a while between seeing each other. But over a period of a year and a half, we fell in love," Linda Warren said.

There was discussion of whether the marriage would work, as combining the two families meant, for Dick, a return to hands-on fatherhood. At this point, Doug was in college and Janice had already married and started a life of her own. But Linda's son Michael was just entering college, and Linda's daughter Jennifer was still just a teenager. "I asked him if he really wanted to do this. His children were grown," Linda said. But nevertheless, in April 1984, the couple married. The location of the wedding was perfect for two people who loved being on the ski slopes more than almost anyplace else. They and their wedding party rode the ski lift to the top of a slope at Gunstock, the ski resort where Linda worked and where Dick asked her on their first date.

With the marriage, changes came to both the Warren and Joyal families. In June 1984, Linda, her thirteen-year-old daughter Jennifer and her eighteen-year-old son Michael moved from Laconia, New Hampshire, to Cape Cod. It was their first introduction to the area and to Four Seas itself, Linda Warren said. "When we were dating, all Richard had told me was that he was a teacher and a guidance counselor and that he ran an ice cream shop in the summertime. I'd never heard of Four Seas, never come to the Cape, so I didn't know what I was getting into."

What she quickly learned was that Four Seas wasn't just any ice cream store. Even in the first few months of their marriage, four days a week Dick Warren was out the door of the home they shared on Hi-ona-Hill Road and off to make ice cream at around five o'clock in the morning. Then, with lines out the door in the evenings, he was often at the store until late at night. A basic inventory of the products that were needed in the fountain area was done on a nightly basis, and a more thorough inventory of essentially everything in the store, from cleaning products to ice cream ingredients, was done every weekend. "It was an awful lot of work," Linda said.

At the time, things were very different at Four Seas than they are now. Four Seas employees were always expected to add up their customers' total bills in their heads rather than use a calculator. But at the time, adding the totals and then inputting them into the antique cash registers that were used was much more difficult for employees—and Linda—to learn. The cash registers were old and wooden and weren't even powered by electricity at the time, a nod to the ice cream store's long history of staying true to its small-town, small-business roots. "If the bill came to, let's say, $12.40, you had to push the $5.00 button two times, the $2.00 button once and then the $0.40 button once," Linda remembers. With her background in accounting and bookkeeping at Gunstock Mountain Resort, Linda quickly settled into the same role at Four Seas. "I was in my glory. What was overwhelming were the people. Richard was so good with them. He could make ice cream and then be out talking to customers, then run back to make the ice cream and then be right back out to talk some more. It was the reason people came to the store. But me, I was happier in my office."

Their new life on Cape Cod changed things for Jennifer and Michael, too. Michael didn't work at Four Seas, choosing to spend his first two summers home from college doing construction and landscaping work on Cape Cod. His junior year, Michael stayed at his college, working as a firefighter at the University of New Hampshire. For Jennifer, it was a tough transition to living on Cape Cod and being expected to work at Four Seas. She said:

> It was very difficult for me. I was thirteen and so I wasn't paying much attention to anybody but myself. It was hell for me, actually. I didn't work at the store the first summer we moved down, but the second I was expected to because you don't have a choice when you're part of the family. And it

Jennifer Joyal, daughter of Linda Warren, worked in the store as a teenager. *Courtesy of the Warren family.*

scared the hell out of me. I can't add. So being in front of people with a bunch of numbers behind you on the wall that you have to add, and a cash register that wasn't automated? No, not for me.

Like most young members of the Warren family, Jennifer spent her early teenage years marking packages, washing dishes and helping with the cleaning of the always-busy store. But after one summer season of waiting on customers, Jennifer began looking for another job, eventually becoming a camp counselor and lifeguard at the local YMCA. However, she was still expected to help when the store was short an employee or when the end of the year rolled around and many Four Seas employees had returned to their off-Cape colleges. It wasn't something she relished. "I only worked behind the counter when they were in desperate need. I'm more than happy to wash dishes, wash ice cream cans, put the dishes away. But I hate waiting on customers."

It was something that Dick, who was often found chatting with customers between making batches of ice cream and performing other chores around the ice cream store, didn't quite understand and something that other young members of the Warren family have struggled with as well. Jennifer said:

I heard that I should suck it up, that I had to at least try. I got all that typical parenting stuff that makes you feel guilty. When you are the child of the person who owns the place, a lot more is expected of you than of other employees. And in my teenage mind, I didn't think that was fair, and I wanted to be judged on my own merit and not because I was part of the family. So that's why I went off and did my own thing.

Though she was less than enthusiastic about being a Four Seas employee, her connection to Dick Warren in his capacity as a teacher and guidance counselor at Barnstable High School was a bit more positive. During all four years of high school, Jennifer would see her stepfather around the school. For many students it might be unnerving, and at times it was, Jennifer said—both her mother and stepfather showed up to chaperone her senior prom. But at least most of the time, the perks outweighed the embarrassing moments. Linda recalls Jennifer being excited that she could visit her stepfather's classroom and sneak gum out of his desk. Jennifer herself remembers getting lunch money from her mother every morning and tricking Dick into giving her more money during the day. "Plus, I basically had a standing hall pass because I could get them from him whenever I wanted," Jennifer said. The teen's relationship with her stepfather "was a love-hate thing."

He was my stepfather. He was my guidance counselor. He followed me wherever I went. However, without him I wouldn't be who I am today. He expected more of me and everybody else who worked at Four Seas than they expected of themselves. There was always that little bit of resentment. But as I look back on it now, I never could have accomplished what I have without him.

A NEW ERA FOR FOUR SEAS

Though Four Seas Ice Cream had an amount of notoriety on Cape Cod and even in some surrounding areas of New England, and the legacy of the Kennedy family enjoying the treat had made the rounds of some tabloid publications, it wasn't until the 1980s and 1990s that the store began receiving more nationwide recognition. Linda Warren recalled:

Four Seas in the Early Warren Years

Cape Cod has always been a tourist area. But to go to Four Seas, you've got to want to go to Four Seas. It's not on the beaten path. So Four Seas was always past patrons telling other people about the store, it was that word of mouth and just a little bit of advertising. Richard had advertisements for the store's opening weekend sale and for the closing sale, but that was it.

Linda began sending press releases to local publications but also to national magazines and newspapers—and the result was mind-blowing, she said. Suddenly, visitors were telling the Warrens they had traveled from New York—or even farther—simply to taste the ice cream. The Warrens, who had always been involved with the trade group the New England Ice Cream Restaurant Association, also joined the National Ice Cream Retailers Association to reach out to other restaurants across the country. It was no longer just locals enjoying the treat and recognizing the Four Seas name. A publicity event in partnership with Coca-Cola in 1988 brought local and regional recognition to the store. As part of its publicity push for a new soda, cherry-flavored 7UP, the Coca-Cola Company partnered with Four Seas to create "the world's largest ice cream float." Three-gallon blocks of Four Seas Ice Cream, about fifty gallons in all, were added to an aboveground swimming pool that was filled with three hundred gallons of cherry 7UP. Brave volunteers in

The Four Seas Ice Cream sign on opening day, which always falls the weekend before Memorial Day. *Courtesy of the Warren family.*

swimsuits could plunge into the pool to dig through the chunks of ice cream for coins that they would trade for prizes. The top winners received $700 in prizes each. It was silly, Linda Warren said, but it brought a lot of recognition to the store. "After about four years, I stopped sending out press releases. I just couldn't do it anymore. But the word got out. Since then, we've been lucky enough every year to get some sort of notoriety, and that keeps the name out there." she said.

Despite recognition from national publications, Four Seas itself was very much the same under Linda and Dick as it had been under Dick and Georgia or even W. Wells Watson. In the late 1980s, the walk-in cooler was expanded and another walk-in freezer, the store's largest, was added. But beyond those structural changes, the store looked much the same as it had decades before, from the old magazine articles and nautical knickknacks decorating the walls to the building itself—which, with every passing year, sunk a bit farther into the sandy ground it was built on, leaving the dining room area slanted. "Nothing was ever supposed to change. When the curtains needed to be replaced, I went out and got the same exact material and made them to look exactly like the curtains Georgia had put in decades before," Linda Warren said. The couple's dedication to its loyal fans continued too.

Regulars were always recognized by employees and the Warrens alike. Many photos of those same regulars and their families grace the walls at Four Seas. And even on the busiest days, groups of preschoolers were still invited to watch the ice cream making process. "Richard used to believe that anything you could show a child, you should. On the wall there used to be all these thank-you cards from the little kids he'd given tours to," Linda said. It's a tradition that continues at Four Seas, with small groups from local preschools visiting every year to learn the magic of ice cream making (and get a sample, of course).

BECOMING AN EXPERT

With national recognition of Four Seas as a place to go for quality ice cream, Dick Warren became well known as the man who kept that legend going. After he had been in the ice cream business for several decades, Richard Warren was frequently asked to do speaking engagements, which quickly grew to requests across the country at restaurant association gatherings. Richard Warren was already well versed in speaking and teaching from his experiences at Barnstable High School. As the head of several speech classes and the high school's speech and debate team, Warren worked on a near-daily basis with students on how to speak in public and even traveled with the debate team to locations across the region. He was even honored years after his retirement with an induction into the Massachusetts Forensic League in 2001. "He was extremely pleased with that," wife Linda said. And her husband "had always been a people person," so it was a natural progression to regular speaking engagements across the country, where Warren would share the history of his little store and the business principles that had kept it operating successfully for so many years. Ice cream retailers and others were always fascinated by Warren's ability to keep the store thriving—and especially its ability to attract employees year after year. Linda Warren, who often accompanied her husband to his speaking engagements, remembered, "Because of the way he kept his help, everybody across the country was so curious. Nobody could keep their help, had turnover, turnover, turnover. But our kids would stay for years and years, even though we were only seasonal and only hired young adults, teenagers. So he became very popular at these conventions."

Out of this, always-chatty Warren gained dozens of new friends and met hundreds of fellow ice cream restaurateurs, as well as an opportunity to share strategies—something he was never afraid to do, Linda said. But he also got a few other things out of the deal. A lifelong skier and golfer who spent every free hour practicing his two favorite sports solo or with friends and Four Seas employee "alumni," Warren would choose where to schedule speaking engagements based, at least in part, on whether a challenging golf course was nearby. "He would pick and choose where he wanted to go. If there was a good golf course close, that's where he wanted to speak," Linda said. The store also benefited from Warren's nationwide speaking engagements. Whatever fee Warren charged for the engagement was donated to the Randall Mark Warren Scholarship Fund.

Once the national recognition of Four Seas and Warren's ability to run the store successfully reached a fever pitch, he and friend Ed Marks, an ice cream flavor salesman, decided to turn their expertise into training for other aspiring ice cream store owners. Along with working at companies that sold the flavorings, extracts and ingredients to other ice cream retailers, Marks had been general manager at three ice cream chains in the 1960s and 1970s: Milk Maid Ice Cream, Amity House and the Penn Supreme Shoppes.

Both men, longtime members of the ice cream industry, belonged to trade organizations, including the New England Ice Cream Restaurant Association and the National Ice Cream Retailers Association. At conventions, "it seemed that people were always asking us questions about how to do this and that and the other thing. So we said, 'Why don't we start a seminar?' It sounded like a good joke, and we laughed about it. But then we went ahead with the plan," Marks said.

Held for the first few years in a hotel in Lancaster, Pennsylvania, the new professors expected a handful of people to show up for the first class. "I think our hope was to have at least twenty people sign up for the first class, and we actually had about twenty-eight," Marks said. After a few years, the class grew to include dozens more people; its most successful year boasted seventy-eight students. "A lot of them were people who were thinking about an ice cream store or those who already had one but needed some help," Linda said. The seminar quickly evolved into a low-key three-day event that was more conversation than instruction. There were no textbooks, no set curriculum and no set class schedule—just two experts chatting about their passion for ice cream retailing. "We just flew by the seat of our pants. After all, the people shared a common dream—to open an ice cream store and make a million bucks. You can't lose, right?"

And in fact, Warren and Marks couldn't lose with that method of teaching their craft. Several years after Successful Ice Cream Retailers started in that hotel conference room, another well-known expert in the field showed up to assess the class for its potential as a seminar at one of the country's most prestigious universities. Known for its Ivy League–level classes, football and school pride, Penn State University in State College, Pennsylvania, is also known in the ice cream community as one of the best places to get a scoop and learn about the business, too. Students in the school's College of Agricultural Sciences operate the Berkey Creamery, which is the country's largest university creamery. They use about four and a half million pounds of milk each year to make ice creams, sherbets, yogurts and cheeses. It's a premier place for undergraduates interested in the restaurant business to learn the trade. Since 1892, Penn State University has also offered a dairy manufacturing program through its School of Agriculture. At the time, it was offered in the winter because farmers and their sons were likely to have more free time in the winter, when farming was at a standstill, than in the spring, summer and fall. By 1925, Penn State had begun offering a class specifically on ice cream production because the dessert treat was so popular nationwide. Much of that had to do with manufacturing becoming cheaper, meaning that more Americans could afford to produce or purchase it. Today, the program is still offered in January because, like farming, ice cream manufacturing and sales are slower in the winter than at any other time of the year. That ten-day program for commercial ice cream makers and retailers always focused on the science, technology and process of making ice cream.

But in the late 1980s, the school decided to expand its class offerings to the retail side of ice cream. The professor who ran the ten-day Penn State ice cream making course from 1985 to 1999, Arun Kilara, approached the duo. Separate from Penn State's how-to seminar on ice cream, Successful Ice Cream Retailing instead focused on Warren and Marks's recommendations on everything from the right type of architecture for an ice cream store to questions related to hiring. Attendees of the class learned, from soup to nuts, exactly how to open an ice cream store; how to staff it and keep it staffed; how to create an identifiable brand; and how to properly price merchandise, among other things. Richard Warren focused on tips and tricks for making tasty ice cream in a batch freezer, which he swore by over the more modern but less hands-on continuous-freeze ice cream makers that many other stores were using. He would recommend recipes, types of ice cream mix and the machines he thought worked best for small ice cream retailers. If Warren and Marks weren't experts in a particular subject, they would bring in as a guest lecturer someone who was, Doug Warren said.

For several years under Professor Kilara, Successful Ice Cream Retailing thrived. But in the early 2000s, things became tense when Kilara left Penn State University to become an independent consultant in the ice cream industry. His replacement just didn't see eye to eye with Warren and Marks, whose laid-back style did not mesh with the rules, regulations and curriculum requirements of Penn State—and which the new head of the ice cream program insisted were followed to the letter. "Where we had been casual in our methods, he demanded that we follow Penn State rules and regulations and procedures. It wasn't fun anymore," Marks said. In his mid-seventies and ready to retire, Marks left two years after Kilara's replacement took over, in 2005. Warren continued teaching the program for a short time before leaving Successful Ice Cream Retailing behind at Penn State.

But it wasn't the end of the class itself; two other colleges, the University of Florida and the University of Wisconsin, expressed interest in hosting the popular seminar. Like Penn State, the University of Wisconsin is known for its dairy program and was the first school in the country to offer classes in dairy production. Its program opened in 1890. The University of Florida called to Warren because around the same time, Linda and Richard Warren began to travel to Florida for vacations and golfing. But the University of Wisconsin and its prestigious dairy program became home for Successful Ice Cream Retailing under the guidance of Warren and one of his first students, Bill Meagher, who took the class in 1994 and opened his own successful ice cream store, Lakeside Creamery in Deep Creek Lake, Maryland, based on what he learned. Around the time Successful Ice Cream Retailing moved to Wisconsin, Richard Warren "wanted to get out of it. We were starting to travel all over the place," Linda said. Meagher and others still run the ice cream class out of the Wisconsin college each year.

Richard Warren's tips for successful restaurant retailing were applicable to other places than just running an ice cream store, son Douglas said. Over the years, Doug ran several other businesses, including a candy store and a pizza and yogurt café. And in every one of them, he found a place for the training his father had instilled in him. He remembers:

> I try to instill my training from Four Seas into everything. One of my dad's most important lessons was that if you take good care of your employees and give them a good work environment, they'll give back to you in spades. At one point, when I was running an eatery in Las Vegas, I would frequently lose employees to other businesses in the same strip mall that offered just two dollars extra per hour in pay. And I told them I couldn't pay them extra but I could guarantee they'd like it with me better. And employees would come back just a few weeks later asking for their old jobs back. They simply just enjoyed what they did.

One of the defining characteristics of Richard Warren's teaching style was that he was unequivocally helpful to anyone—even potential competitors. Over the years of teaching Successful Ice Cream Retailing, several Cape Cod ice cream store owners and those attempting to get a Cape Cod ice cream store off the ground attended the course, "but he wasn't so competitive that he wouldn't help out," son Doug said. One store still features a Four Seas Ice Cream signature that Dick suggested would add a personal touch: photos on the wall of summer employees from over the years, a tradition started in the 1950s at Four Seas and continued to this day. He would even help those store owners develop recipes and would point them in the direction of the manufacturers of his favorite flavors and products, Doug said. He did keep some things secret, though, such as exact proportions of flavors.

ICE SCREAMERS

As Dick Warren's notoriety in the ice cream business grew, his passion for the collectibles dedicated to the sweet treat grew and grew. Georgia Thomas (then Warren) had collected antique Victorian ice cream molds, a popular way for ice cream to be served in the early 1900s. The ice cream would be softened and then pressed into cast-metal molds in hundreds of different shapes for various occasions. There were roses and daisies for ladies' teas, toy shapes for children and even unique molds such as ocean liners for special occasions. That collection was eventually passed to Peggy Warren, Doug Warren's wife and business partner.

But Dick took the collecting to a much higher level. In the beginning, his collection stemmed from scouring antiques shops and mail-order collectibles catalogues for ice cream scoops, from modern scoops that would be used at Four Seas to those dating back hundreds of years. Four Seas, in fact, uses a triangular-shaped scoop for its medium ice cream cone. It's one of the only stores, if not the only store, that still uses the antique scoops. They are no longer made, and many still used at the store today were purchased during Dick's collecting years, when he would pay

Richard and Linda Warren at an Ice Screamers collectibles convention. *Courtesy of the Warren family.*

upward of $100 for one of the unique antiques. In the 1980s, Dick joined the Ice Screamers, an ice cream collectibles group started by Ed Marks in 1982. "He became one of the earliest members," Marks, author of the book *Ice Cream Collectibles*, said. The two men had known each other for decades prior, since Marks worked at a company that sold ice cream flavorings—though Dick, who was "almost paranoid" about changing his flavors even slightly and upsetting his customers, never bought those flavorings, Marks said.

Marks moved from Springfield, Massachusetts, to Pennsylvania in 1968, but the two men continued to meet up with each other at meetings of the New England Ice Cream Restaurant Association and National Ice Cream Retailers Association, of which both were members. And when Warren joined the Ice Screamers, his collecting took off. From scoops, Dick moved on to collecting other items used in ice cream shops around the country, from milkshake machines—known as frappes in the New England states— to antique signs and sundae dishes. Ice cream makers for home use, from modern automated machines to those requiring at least a half hour of cranking to create the frozen treat, rounded out the early collection. Again, that wasn't enough, and Dick began collecting essentially anything mentioning ice cream or with an ice cream photo, including postcards, old photographs, advertisements, fliers and even Victorian valentines. Some of the most interesting items in his collection were pens, knives, hats and some "penny licks," shot glass–like dishes that were sold to ice cream consumers for a penny apiece. The glasses were filled with ice cream and then given back to the vendor to be washed, filled with ice cream again and sold to someone who wanted just a taste of ice cream or couldn't afford any more. Son Doug remembered:

> *Basically anything that had anything to do with ice cream, he would buy it. He started to get really interested in anything having to do with the history of the ice cream-making process. At first, there wasn't eBay. But when eBay came around, he learned from his stepson Michael and son-in-law Steve, my sister Janice's husband, how to use that. I think it's the only reason he got into computers at all, to buy and sell his stuff. Otherwise I don't think he would have embraced computers at all.*

In July 1991, the Centerville Historical Museum, located just around the corner from Four Seas on Main Street in Centerville, featured an exhibit of some of Dick Warren's ice cream memorabilia, from some of those original scoops to some of the ice cream mogul's personal favorites. It featured scoops, home ice cream makers and some of his penny licks glasses dating from over the eighteenth and nineteenth centuries. Many of the first ice cream scoops were Gilcrest scoops from the 1920s, a popular scoop for home ice cream consumption, as well as a few from the 1800s that required two hands to use—one hand to hold the scoop and another to turn a knob that pushed the ice cream out of the scoop. One of his most prized finds displayed in the museum's show was a Philadelphia frappe maker from the 1890s purchased for $60 and later appraised at more than $1,000. The machine used cranks to make two frappe cups move up and down like pistons to mix ice cream with milk and flavorings. Though the exhibit showcased some of Warren's unique and favorite collectibles, it was "just the tip of the iceberg" when it came to the whole collection, Centerville Historical Museum curator Nancy Lee Nelson said in a 1991 *Cape Cod Times* article. The show featured seventy-five of Warren's collectibles. His collection? It featured two thousand items.

The Warrens' passion for collecting ice cream memorabilia extended to their home. Doug remembers a board full of ice cream scoops that graced the kitchen wall when he was growing up in the Centerville home, and the Warrens' Christmas tree each year was decorated mainly with ice cream–themed ornaments. Always, a few depictions of Four Seas itself by local artists were included in their home. And visitors to the home were happily shown parts of the collection, such as the framed magazine covers depicting old-time soda jerks or the tiny Victorian Valentine's Day cards that graced hallways. Friends and fellow collectors Patty and Thor Foss, who edit the Ice Screamers' newsletter, remember a visit when Warren's collection yielded a prized and beloved postcard from Patty's childhood:

> *We made a stop to see Dick and Linda, and Dick wanted to show us where lots of his collection was kept, which was all over the house. In the living room, he showed us a number of trunks that were loaded with paper collectibles. Dick told us to make ourselves at home, so we sat down on the floor and really got into checking out the many trade cards. All of a sudden, we spotted a soda fountain trade card that advertised a soda fountain from my home town in Keyport, New Jersey. What a surprise; I couldn't believe it. We're here in Massachusetts and we saw a card from Keyport.*

With membership in the Ice Screamers came conferences across the country. At these events, collectors would bring their memorabilia to buy, sell and trade with others, but for many of the Ice Screamers, it was the socialization and entertainment after trading that made the shows worthwhile. Some of that entertainment came from Dick Warren himself. Ever an entertainer who wanted his friends and customers to have a good laugh, Warren often made speeches at the collectibles conventions dressed in his ice cream finest—which often included an ice cream–patterned shirt or tie, topped off with a hat shaped like, yes, an ice cream cone. Some of his zaniest antics came when he teamed up with another ice cream memorabilia collector for what Ice Screamers still call the *Dick and John Show*. Along with Ice Screamer John Panza, who sold ice cream flavorings for many stores on the East Coast, Dick put on a show every year, including an ice cream tasting. But unlike traditional ice cream tastings, which include new flavors or new versions of old favorites, the stars of the *Dick and John Show* made sure to shock their friends with the strangest and, sometimes, most unpalatable ice cream flavors they could come up with. Mixed in to the six flavors they would make at home and bring to the conventions were savory flavors such as tomato or garlic. "They would bring about six terrible flavors for us to taste. A lot of our Screamers actually enjoyed them, though I always told both of them they were terrible," Ed Marks said. Another year, a prune Danish–flavored ice cream was produced for the convention attendees to sample. And in true tongue-in-cheek style, Dick "told everyone he would be handing out Maalox at the end of his presentation," Patty Foss said. Though the Ice Screamers tried them good-naturedly, everyone acknowledged that some of the stranger flavors never had a chance of being scooped at Four Seas or anywhere else, for that matter.

But interestingly, some of Dick Warren's strangest concoctions did make it into his 2006 guide to ice cream making at home, *The Complete Idiot's Guide to Homemade Ice Cream*. The flavors featured both his perennial conference favorites, tomato and garlic, plus a sampling of other vegetable and spice flavors like jalapeno, sweet potato, oatmeal, the Victorian-era rose petal and mincemeat. When Warren worked on his book, friends and family were again "treated" to these unique flavors as he revamped them for home ice cream maker use.

A Transition

Though Richard Warren's passion for ice cream never waned, in the mid-1990s, he and Linda began considering moving toward retirement from Four Seas, though they would always have a hand in it. They had begun traveling more—frequently to visit Four Seas Ice Cream's former employees, always known at the store as "alumni"—and were ready to hand the reins over. But the process of transitioning the store to its third owners, Warren's son Douglas and his wife Peggy, was years in the making.

Chapter 3
GROWING UP FOUR SEAS

Stories from Members of the "Four Seas Family"

Four Seas Ice Cream isn't just unique because of the way its ice cream is made or for its ability to stand the test of time and remain an old-fashioned ice cream parlor, from its flavors to its decorations. Ask many customers and they'll tell you the ice cream is nice, but what makes Four Seas truly special are the people who work there year after year, serving up a smile with the sundaes and cones. And employees will tell you that the traditions that have been carried through the decades make Four Seas just as memorable of a place to work as it was decades ago.

It wasn't for nothing that Richard Warren became known in the ice cream retailers' community for his hiring practices at Four Seas Ice Cream. His practices are still used to this day at Four Seas and were perfected over the decades. Though unorthodox, they've led to loyal employees who return summer after summer, some through both high school and college. They've led to decades-long friendships between employees, a special bond between the owners and the teens who serve the thousands of ice cream cones every year—and even to marriages. Several couples have met while working at Four Seas and eventually married. Others met their spouses when one was working at the ice cream store and the other was a customer. And much of the camaraderie and bonding that goes on each and every summer can be traced to the unique hiring practices of the Warren family at Four Seas.

ONLY THE BEST

In early spring, still months from when Four Seas Ice Cream officially opens for the summer season, employees are already being considered for jobs behind the counter, in the sandwich kitchen and ice cream room and as cleaners and dishwashers. And while many employees are considered for their jobs based on résumés listing past experience, Richard Warren—and now Doug Warren—always turned to a different piece of paper to determine who would be best to work at the bustling Four Seas every summer: a notecard. Each year, a member of the Warren family visits Barnstable High School to bring notecards to the teachers of sophomore honors-level courses in every subject. The goal isn't to find out who might be good at math, for example, or an accomplished public speaker in drama class. Instead, teachers are asked to nominate the three male and three female students in their classes whom the instructors believe would be best suited for the fast-paced job. In the nearly three decades when Richard Warren was an English teacher, speech and debate coach and guidance counselor at Barnstable High School, he would simply deliver the index cards to his fellow teachers in their classrooms. Doug Warren, who substitute taught and later taught full time at the same school, did the same during his years as an instructor.

An employee tradition is for employees of over three summers to write their names on the wall above the dishwashing area. *Photo by Jennifer Badalamenti/Roots Workshop.*

But their lack of a full-time presence at Barnstable High School hasn't diminished teachers' enthusiasm for helping pick Four Seas' next employees. At this point, veteran teachers know to expect the notecards every year, and new teachers are quickly made wise to their arrival and participate enthusiastically (they also receive a few quarts of ice cream as a thank-you). They look for special qualities that Four Seas employees need to have in order to be successful at the job, mainly: a hardworking attitude, outgoing personality, excitement about learning new skills and the ability to multitask in a very bustling setting. Students who work at Four Seas have also always been required to keep honor roll–level grades, and many of them do that in honors and college-level classes while fulfilling roles in the school play or acting as president of their chosen club or church group. The nominated students are then called and, if they're interested in the job, are invited for an interview.

In the past two decades, since Richard Warren retired from education in 1988, the selection has expanded to include some students who don't go to Barnstable High School. With students starting school earlier on Cape Cod than in previous years, the store needs its employees to continue working into September, and typically only those from private schools or schools in other regions are able to do so. Many of these employees are longtime summer residents of the Centerville area and grew up going to Four Seas as a special summer treat. There has never been a lack of interested students. "There was a little bit of envy among my friends and the friends of other people who worked there. Working at Four Seas was kind of a status symbol," Dave LeMarbre, an employee from 1967 until the late 1970s and longtime friend of Richard and Linda Warren, said. But in order to make the very popular jobs accessible to other students than those at Barnstable High, a few "résumés"—typically, a handwritten, heartfelt letter detailing why they'd like to work at Four Seas and why they would be a good match for the job—are accepted every year. But even those students must prove they're the right type of person for the job—and in a very specific way. According to Linda Warren: "Parents would call and ask how their kids could get a job. And Richard would tell them to have the child write a letter and he would get back to them then, and only then. And if no letter came, they didn't get considered for a job. And if the parents wrote the letter or accompanied a student on an interview, they didn't get the job."

But though the types of employees hired have changed over the years, the expectations for them have not. The job, Douglas Warren said, just isn't for everyone. "If you aren't willing to work, you're not going to do well here,"

An employee suits up to stock the store's freezers with quarts and pints. *Photo by Jennifer Badalamenti/Roots Workshop.*

he said. To explain that sentiment, Richard Warren often shared a favorite quotation with employees struggling to find the motivation to work hard. "My dad always said, 'If there's time to lean there's time to clean,' and we still remind the kids of that all the time."

Four Seas employees are expected to do much more than many teens with summer jobs. Until the past few decades, all employees worked double shifts several times a week, meaning they arrived early in the morning, took a short break for dinner and returned to the shop later in the evening to stay until closing. Doug remembers:

> *There were only four people on a shift, and you would work with the same group. And there were literally ten people working there in the early years. You would work three days, then two nights, then have a day or two off… Everybody worked mega amounts of hours. The managers were expected to work fifty hours, and you didn't get paid overtime.*

The number of employees working at Four Seas each summer has grown exponentially. Even today, many employees practice the same work ethic, picking up extra shifts for one another and staying late to make the shop spotless for the next crop of workers coming in the morning. The work expected of employees—who range in age from fourteen to college-aged twentysomethings who have returned to work at the store for years—begins nearly two months before Four Seas Ice Cream opens for the scooping season. In early April, employees begin spending their weekends working in the shop, preparing it for the summer, and many spend their spring breaks doing the same thing. "Preseason" jobs are messy and unglamorous—sanding down walls, waxing windows, painting chairs and scrubbing freezers are par for the course, often for hours at a time. The work goes on, usually, until just hours before Four Seas opens for the season the Saturday before Memorial Day, as it has opened since the days when W. Wells Watson operated the shop.

It's a good introduction for the employees, and it isn't the last time they'll spend hours scrubbing from floor to ceiling. Each evening after Four Seas closes, employees stay at work at least an extra half hour in order to prepare for the next morning. And once a month, the practice known as "chest cleaning" occurs, as it has since nearly the beginning of the store's inception. After the ice cream store closes for the night, usually around 10:30 p.m., all of the store's employees gather at the store to scrub everything from top to bottom, dragging chairs out to be washed, scrubbing floors—with toothbrushes sometimes—and generally erasing the grime that thousands of feet attached to thousands of customers can create. A late night, employees usually return home in the early hours of the morning, with many up just a few hours later to begin their regular shift the next day. And again at the end of the year, Four Seas finishes up with a "closing day sale"—and yet more cleaning to ready the store for the vacant winter ahead. "You just really get down to cleaning, get dirty and disgusting with all these other employees," Doug said.

In Warren's days, chest cleaning nights were capped off by parties at the store. "My dad basically turned a blind eye to us having a few drinks at the store. We would just sit there and play games, talk, just help each other out. Chief trusted us, and nobody ever broke that trust. It was a simple time," he said. Employees are no longer allowed to spend after-hours time at the store. But though Four Seas no longer serves as a party spot for employees, employees are rewarded in other ways for their hard, sometimes grimy, work. Throughout the summer and even into the winter, employees are provided with incentives to work hard and come back each year, beginning with the annual after-hours pool party midway through the season, followed by a closing-day party the weekend after Labor Day when the fountain officially closes for the winter. That tradition was started by W. Wells Watson, who took his employees out to a fine dining restaurant each year in appreciation. According to Doug:

> *In the middle of the summer, when people are getting stressed out and the days are long, the employees need something to get them laughing and enjoying themselves again. So we have a pool party to share stories about work and customers, and to have time to commiserate with each other. And then the closing day party is also special. There's a big hoo-rah when you sell the last quart, and then you leave at 5:30 and at 6:15 you're expected to be ready and at the restaurant. There's such a transformation. We see these kids all year long in ponytails, no makeup, no jewelry, no frills. And then all of a sudden we get to see everybody as they actually are.*

The employee incentives don't end there. Every year, the first weekend in January, employees are treated to an all-expenses-paid ski trip to New

As a thank-you to their employees, Four Seas Ice Cream owners take their employees on an all-expenses-paid ski trip in the winter. *Courtesy of the Warren family.*

Hampshire as a thank-you for their hard work the previous summer. The tradition began in the 1960s, after Richard and Georgia Warren purchased a small cabin near Gunstock Mountain Resort, a longtime favorite ski destination for the couple and their young growing family. For over three decades, the ski "camp" served as home base for the Four Seas employees who came up to ski during the day and enjoy dinners and movies together in the evening. As Richard became more interested in skiing ever more difficult mountains, he and wife Linda made the decision in 1998 to sell the camp. "He didn't want to ski up there anymore. It was too little. He wanted to ski the big mountains, so we sold it and he'd stay at a hotel near the places he wanted to ski," Linda said. But it wasn't the end of the ski trip for employees. Today, Doug and Peggy Warren still rent a cabin near Gunstock Mountain in the town of Gilford, New Hampshire.

Making Friends and Keeping Them

There is a phrase bandied about frequently among Four Seas Ice Cream employees and former employees: "You know you're a Four Seas employee when you wake up the morning after your shift stuck to your sheets with hot fudge." But the silly sentiment extends much further than that; it also applies to the friendships and other bonds formed by hard work and long hours at the ice cream shop, as well as the time Four Seas employees spend with one another outside of work. Because of the closeness of working behind a cramped soda fountain counter for hours on end, employees become very close very quickly and often spend their off-hours enjoying the Centerville area's beaches, restaurants and outdoor activities like kayaking and swimming. Many employees also keep in touch between summers while they are away at college or in different high schools—in the earlier days by letter and today frequently by online means. "My favorite thing about Four Seas is the camaraderie, watching the kids just blend together no matter if they would have hung out outside of work. They would be there in a second if you needed them or if they needed each other," Linda Warren said.

That closeness also means employees are very comfortable with one another—and comfortable poking fun at one another too, in the form of pranks and "initiations" that have taken place every summer nearly since Four Seas' opening in 1934. "It's kind of a 'welcome to our club' sort of thing. It means now you're one of us, now you're part of the team, the Four Seas family," Doug Warren said. Those welcomes have included everything

Employees scoop up summertime treats. *Photo by Jennifer Badalamenti/Roots Workshop.*

from dousings with water and flour to employees being soaked in water and thrown in the freezer—though it's done at the end of a person's shift so they can promptly go home and change, Warren said. Recently, the Warrens themselves have gotten in on the fun, helping more experienced employees play a good-hearted prank on younger ones by sending them to the motel across the street with a three-gallon tub of ice cream "to go." They're sent to various rooms with the ice cream but are then relieved by older coworkers and told it's been a joke. "Somebody ended up in a trash can once, somebody else in the sink. But it really creates this sort of community," Four Seas co-owner and Doug's wife Peggy Warren said.

Sometimes, employees team up to play pranks on one another or even other members of the community. There have been fights played out with whipped cream, buckets of caramel and spoonfuls of ice cream on rainy, unpopular early season days. Employees' cars have been covered in marshmallow cream and silly signs, and once, a particular customer who insisted on parking his boat in the parking lot on especially crowded evenings received a dose of the same medicine. "There was a kid who would park his boat in the parking lot, and it would always be dirty and smell of fish. And this guy would just always give Chief a hard time and throw parts of the

An employee goofing off in the 1970s. This employee's two sons also went on to work at Four Seas. *Courtesy of the Warren family.*

fish he'd cleaned into our dumpsters. So we decided that if he was going to stink up our parking lot, we would do the same to his boat. So we put fish in a plastic bag on a Friday afternoon, and he didn't use the boat until a week later. He called the police, but we just had such a laugh. But we didn't tell Chief. That was the kind of crazy stuff we did," former employee Dave LeMarbre said.

Though much of the Four Seas camaraderie centers on good-natured pranks and jokes, it has taken a more serious, romantic turn in the past. Richard and Georgia Warren were not the only couple to meet at Four Seas, fall in love during their summers working together and eventually get married. By the Warren family's count, there have been at least four other marriages that have occurred because of a bond created at Four Seas. For years, employee Saunie Chase, who began working under W. Wells Watson in the summer of 1957 at age thirteen, had giggled alongside other Four Seas employees when handsome young men came into the store. She and the other girls would create special sundaes and frappes for their favorite customers, packing as much ice cream and as many toppings into their concoctions as they could under Watson's watchful eye. But in 1962, when Chase was eighteen, she finally caught the eye of a customer she had paid special attention to since she began working at Four Seas. Saunie Chase Canuso remembers:

> *In the summer of 1962, Marshall Reilly came in and wanted to know how old I was. I told him I was eighteen and he said, "Now I can date you." I'd been waiting for that for five years! We were married in December of 1962, and had two daughters. One filled in at Four Seas before school ended and the other worked at Four Seas for two or three summers.*

Dave LeMarbre and his wife, Trisha, didn't meet at Four Seas Ice Cream, but it's where their love for each other—in addition to their love for Cape Cod and the Warren family—blossomed. In 1966, LeMarbre was a recent transplant to Cape Cod from Marlborough, Massachusetts, when he was asked by Richard Warren to work at Four Seas. He started at the bottom, in the position of morning boy. At later points in his time at Four Seas, he was in charge of making ice cream and helping out one day each week making sandwiches at lunchtime. By the time he left for college at Tennessee Tech University in Cookeville in 1970, LeMarbre was established at Four Seas as one of Warren's trusted nighttime managers, who oversaw operations on the store's busiest nights. It was there that he met Trish, who was also attending the college to study education. LeMarbre continued to work summers at Four Seas, but by 1973, he and Trish were inseparable and planning to marry that December. Trish worked just a few weeks at Four Seas that summer, but the couple returned the next summer and again in 1975, when they were off summers from the teaching positions they had secured in Tennessee. That was the year that the LeMarbres got really close. Trying to save money and help out Richard Warren, they elected to spend the summer living in the Crow's Nest, the attic space of Four Seas. "It was kind of neat for two reasons. The price was right, Chief didn't charge me anything. And he felt a little bit of security because there was always somebody there if something happens," Dave remembers. Trish has a few other memories about the experience:

> *It was crazy. And it was hot as the dickens up there. We had just the front room, and you can barely stand in there. There was a shower up there, but we had to go down to the store to use the bathroom. But David was there almost all the time because he was managing and making ice cream, so it*

made sense. And every morning the morning boys would stick their heads in the door when they came upstairs to get supplies for the store and would make a joke out of it and yell, "Everybody decent?" as loud as they could.

Nevertheless, it didn't give the couple negative memories of Four Seas. They and dozens of other Four Seas alumni keep in touch years after they worked at the ice cream store. It's a testament to how Richard Warren ran the business: as the patriarch of a family, not the head of a bustling summer business. "He was a father figure not just to me but to a lot of kids," Dave LeMarbre said. Richard and Georgia Warren went to LeMarbre's wedding to Trish in Tennessee, and the couple in turn visited Cape Cod the year Randy Warren, their son, died. Rather than wane after years and miles separated them, the bond the two families forged while at Four Seas grew stronger. "We would always visit Massachusetts because Dave's family was there. And we would visit Chief and Linda for the weekend. But Chief would say, 'If you're just coming for the weekend, don't bother coming.' So it would get longer and longer," Trisha said. When Dave LeMarbre's father moved to New Hampshire and eventually fell into ill health and passed away, Chief became an even bigger part of the LeMarbres' life. The two men began visiting each other frequently, with the LeMarbres bringing their two children to Cape Cod and Richard going to Tennessee to spend time at their home there. And Dave began visiting the Warrens in Florida, where they chose to retire. Like working at Four Seas, those experiences were done at Warren's pace, Dave said:

One time I visited him in Florida to play golf for a few days, and his arm was in a sling. He'd cracked his elbow rollerblading. The doctor in the emergency room told him that when he walked into the examination room, he was shocked to find Chief, not some teenage boy. Another time, my sons and I went golfing with him. They were in great shape, so the three of them walked the course. And I'm in the cart looking like a wuss. But after a little while, I thought those boys were going to die. It was ninety-something degrees, tons of humidity. But he just kept trudging along. And later at the beach, we were done. We just stretched out to nap. But he hopped in the water for a four-mile swim. We were amazed. Who was this guy?

That spark for life and dedication to fostering relationships kept Four Seas employees in touch with one another and with the Warren family over the years. "I kept in touch with Dick and Georgia over the years. We played golf together, and they would visit me in Florida. And every time I am on the Cape to visit family, we make it a point to go into Four Seas to say hi and have some ice cream," Saunie Chase Canuso said. In fact, Richard made it a point to visit as many former employees as possible in his travels for speaking engagements, the Successful Ice Cream Retailing course and on his treks to various skiing and golfing destinations across the United States and several other countries. If his travels came even vaguely close to where an alumnus was attending college or living, you could be sure Warren would do his best to visit. And high school students living just a few minutes from him were pretty much guaranteed a very loud, enthusiastic fan at their sports games. The employees have returned the favor, especially in the last few years as the local high school has started its academic year earlier. When this occurs, former employees—from those who just graduated college to many who worked at the ice cream store in the 1970s, '80s and '90s—return to work in the same positions they worked as teenagers. "To have people in their thirties, forties and fifties drop everything to come back and work for you and love it, it's unbelievable. It's amazing that they care so much to help like that," Linda Warren said.

In fact, one of Richard Warren's greatest memories of Four Seas involved the bond he and his Four Seas "family" forged over the years, Linda said. In 1987, the Warrens spent months tracking down "every single" employee to invite them to an alumni reunion, Linda said. The weekend-long event included family picnics and softball games, as well as dinner-dances at a golf club in the town of Sandwich, just a few miles from Centerville. Of course, the event featured Four Seas Ice Cream and two ice cream cakes made by Doug Warren. And neither she nor her husband could believe the enthusiastic response, she said:

> *The response was marvelous, just to a note we sent asking if people were interested. And so we planned our reunion. Out of 133 alumni from the time Richard had run the store, 129 came. That doesn't include their spouses, just the alumni. Only 4 couldn't come. Isn't that amazing? And they came from all over the world. And Richard was right in his glory. My God, if you could see him! He was dancing up a storm, talking up a storm, and there were people all over the place. They came back for Chief and because of the memories and the friendships. And that's pretty special.*

It wasn't the only time that hundreds of Warren's friends, family and supporters gathered to fête the Four Seas patriarch. In 2004, the ice cream

Former employees dressing in Richard "Chief" Warren's signature vintage T-shirt and apron combination, which he wore every morning to make hundreds of gallons of Four Seas Ice Cream. *Courtesy of the Warren family.*

store celebrated its seventieth anniversary, and another party was planned, this one to celebrate both the store's seven decades of business as well as Warren's retirement. And in true Richard Warren style, the party made him the center of attention, with speeches "roasting" him and his quirks, as well as a parade of former employees dressed in some of the uniforms Four Seas employees wore over the years. As a final touch, three alumni— including LeMarbre—donned prosthetic bald caps, white pants, aprons and a particular style of vintage Four Seas T-shirt to visit tables dressed as Chief. "He was getting made fun of, but it was so touching. You could tell it was really nice to be able to enjoy that and have that moment. It was his extended family from across the years and he just loved them all, whether they were joking with him or not," Doug Warren said.

Chapter 4

A CONTINUING FAMILY LEGACY

From One Warren to the Next

In the mid-1990s, Richard and Linda Warren began discussing transitioning from full-time ownership of Four Seas Ice Cream to a more advisory role in the business, both on the ice cream making side that Richard had always run and the bookkeeping aspect that Linda had helmed. When Randy Warren died in the early 1980s, the family's plan for the future of the business was thrown for a loop. It had always been assumed by the Warren family that Randy—who had inherited his father's friendly personality but competitive, hardworking nature— would take over the ice cream store when his parents chose to retire. Richard Warren had always discussed the possibility of opening a second Four Seas location somewhere on Cape Cod, and that store would most likely have gone to younger son Douglas Warren. It had been discussed that Doug could take over the business eventually, but his father also found it very important that his living son forged his own way in life, Doug said. However, with Randy's death, Richard shifted his hopes to his younger son. That encouragement meant that when Linda and Richard decided to begin seriously considering retirement, Doug was no longer living on Cape Cod and was in fact three thousand miles away running another restaurant.

Same Traditions, Different Locations

Douglas Warren graduated from high school in 1981 and then spent a couple of years at the University of Lowell, now known as the University of Massachusetts–Lowell, before transferring to Northern Essex Community College, where he received his degree in mechanical engineering, in line with his dreams to become an architect or designer. Less than a year later, he married his college sweetheart, Heather, and moved to Yarmouth, Maine, before settling in Bowdoinham, Maine. Though his original plans included a job in architecture or another type of design, the influence of Four Seas asserted itself even when Doug was several states away. While Heather worked as a bank teller and eventually a bank branch manager, Doug Warren began applying for jobs in the restaurant and ice cream businesses, receiving offers from a chain of ice cream stores and a diner-style restaurant. In an unexpected move—to him and others—Warren picked the diner. "I figured I should get some more experience than just making ice cream and serving ice cream, so I decided on that restaurant over the ice cream store," he said. But quickly, he realized that the diner wasn't for him either. Managers seemed to be more in charge of manning the grill than handling the dining room, so Doug swiftly left the restaurant. After a short stint selling computers, he landed as a candy maker at Haven's Candies, a popular Maine candy store founded in 1915. His experience making ice creams and toppings came in handy at the candy store, which made its own treats from chocolate truffles to roasted nuts to hand-pulled candy canes during the holiday season. It took just two weeks for Doug's experience from Four Seas to pay off at Haven's. He was promoted to the store's head candy maker over his current manager and another employee who had worked at the store for decades. Doug said:

> And when I used what I learned at Four Seas, the work ethic totally changed. Before, they would even smoke in the candy-making area. But it became a very clean-cut place when I took over. I learned all facets of candy-making, even handling the chocolates that have just come out of the enrobing machine. Usually it's only women who do that job because their body temperature is lower and they won't leave fingerprints on the fresh chocolates, but I was somehow able to do it. In the years I was there, we increased candy production over 30 percent.

But Haven's Candies wasn't Doug Warren's final destination. Frustrated with the lack of ability to move up higher in the management chain, he jumped on an offer to move to Las Vegas, Nevada, to run a café in an outlet mall being constructed on the outskirts of town. The property included several outlet shops and Main Street Eatery, the pizza, sandwich and frozen yogurt café Doug was to run. So in 1993, the couple and their one-and-a-half-year-old son, Joshua, moved to Las Vegas. There, Doug's only connection to ice cream was a soft-serve frozen yogurt machine that served up the trendy, lower-fat concoction. By 1995, though, the outlet mall had closed and, along with it, Main Street Eatery. In the same year, when Josh was three, Heather and Doug Warren divorced, and Doug again moved away from the restaurant business, working a series of sales jobs for two years. It wouldn't be long before Four Seas again came into his life, though it would be another several years before Doug officially moved back to Cape Cod to become the third owner of Four Seas.

In 1997, Richard Warren came to Las Vegas to visit and brought a proposition with him: Doug could take over Four Seas Ice Cream in a few years. "He was thinking about retirement, and Doug was in a good position to maybe take over. He always knew Douglas was going to take over the store, and so Richard decided to propose the plan and then retire in three or four years," Linda Warren said. On that same visit, Richard met another person who would become pivotal to Four Seas' operation: Peggy Wysocki, a single mother with one daughter who had lived in Las Vegas for most of her life, whom Doug began dating in early 1996. The couple met once at a friend's home but didn't speak again until nearly a year later, when Doug brought son Joshua to a New Year's Eve party for children at Peggy's house. Several hours and confetti fights with their kids later, the two exchanged phone numbers. Phone conversations followed for two weeks, and finally a first date was scheduled. By 1997, when Richard visited, the couple had discussed marriage and knew that it was in their future. "I had to convince Peggy to marry me. I'd asked her a couple of times at that point," Doug joked. Richard went back to Cape Cod with a plan to crunch the numbers to decide what purchasing the business, equipment and property would cost Doug and Peggy. By the spring of 1998, a vacation to Centerville was scheduled, and the couple and their two children headed to Cape Cod. It was the first time Peggy had ever been to New England, as well as her first time meeting many of Doug's family members and seeing the quaint town where he grew up. It was also the time when the couple's final decision of whether to move to Cape Cod to take over Four Seas Ice Cream from Doug's father would be made. According to Peggy:

Four Seas Ice Cream on a typical summer night. *Courtesy of Studio by the Sea.*

It was April, so Four Seas wasn't open. So I wasn't able to see the store or taste the ice cream. I'd never done any of it. But I knew it was something that Doug always wanted. He grew up in the business, and it was always in the back of his mind that if Chief retired, he hoped he would get the opportunity to run it. Ice cream runs through his veins like blood. But I didn't really have any preconceived notions about Four Seas at that point. I had no idea what it would be like running it. But I think now that if he'd explained everything to me or if I'd seen it for the first time in the summer, it would have been a little bit daunting to know what kind of responsibility it is. But I just went for it. I put it in God's hands and if it was going to work out, it would.

The next year was a whirlwind. The couple began making final plans to move to Cape Cod and purchase Four Seas. The decision meant months of planning a move, selling Peggy's home, taking their children out of school and driving three thousand miles across the country in the middle of the summer. "It was a very difficult decision. It meant moving out of state, resigning from a position I loved, selling my home. But I also thought of it as an opportunity to own a business, something I'd probably never be able to do otherwise," Peggy said. The couple was also planning a wedding—Doug proposed, and Peggy had finally accepted. The ceremony was scheduled to be held in Las Vegas in the spring of 1999, just a short time before Doug would travel to Cape Cod to work with his father for the summer, learning the ropes of ownership. But an unexpected surgery meant the wedding couldn't happen, and it was shelved for several months. In April 1999, Doug Warren instead set out for Massachusetts, driving a moving truck with many of the couple's possessions in the back and the family's Cairn terrier riding up front.

That summer, Doug Warren worked side by side with his father. When Doug was a teenager, he and his father had made ice cream together. But this time around, the mentorship went further, with ice cream making joined by lessons in pricing, inventorying merchandise, how to handle employees and how to generally keep things running at the ice cream store, which on its busy nights attracts several thousand customers. It was strenuous, hard work, Doug said.

> *We were pretty close. But that first year I came back, he was trying to prove to me how hard he had to work. So even after making ice cream and talking about the business, he would try to stay and wash dishes or clean off tables. He was very nervous but I think very excited and very proud that I was*

Four Seas Ice Cream current owners Peggy and Douglas Warren. *Courtesy of the Warren family.*

From left: Richard "Chief" Warren, son Doug Warren and daughter-in-law Peggy Warren celebrate Four Seas Ice Cream's seventieth anniversary and Richard's retirement. *Courtesy of the Warren family.*

taking over the family legacy. It was understandable. This was close to fifty years of his life. He met his first wife here, raised his children here. It gets in your blood, being around this place.

Peggy arrived that August with her daughter and the family's two cats, having traveled cross-country in a Jeep packed with the rest of the couple's possessions. She began learning how to handle the bookkeeping and accounting for the ice cream store, as Linda Warren had done since the early 1980s. Finally, the couple's long-planned wedding occurred. After a week of forecasts predicting a possible hurricane that weekend, the couple instead woke on September 18, 1999, to a beautiful, sunny day. They were married on Craigville Beach, "just a quarter mile from Four Seas in the place that Chief would swim a mile a day," Doug said.

The struggles surrounding Four Seas weren't over for the newlywed couple, however. The family had decided on a purchasing plan for Doug and Peggy Warren to use to take over the ice cream store. In the first seven years of their ownership, the couple would pay off the purchase of the name "Four Seas Ice Cream" and the store's equipment and then spend the next seven purchasing the building itself and the land it sits on.

A Continuing Family Legacy

Doug and Peggy Warren became co-owners of the business, with each taking a 50 percent share. While that agreement was cordial, convincing a bank to provide such a large loan to the recently relocated couple proved challenging. Doug initially thought that approaching a bank Four Seas had used for decades would mean the exchange would "essentially be a handshake deal. And if anything should be a handshake deal, this should have been," he said. But with no collateral and a hope to purchase a home in the near future as well, a bank Four Seas had used for decades as its main financial institution said no. Several other banks did as well. Several days later, Doug and Peggy had arranged to borrow the money from Linda when the bank called back to say it had reconsidered because of the company's long history of serving Four Seas. But the deal was done, Doug said.

With the transition came the decision of how to announce to family, friends and current and former employees that Richard Warren, who had been at the store since the mid-1950s, and his wife Linda, whose presence at the store began in the mid-1980s, were no longer running the ice cream store. Though the store stayed in the family, there was still some concern that without Chief in the building, many longtime customers would worry about changes for the negative with a younger owner. And the younger Warren couple felt the concern was warranted. "There are plenty of businesses where sons or daughters take over the business and run it into the ground or make so many changes it becomes unrecognizable. That certainly wasn't something we wanted to do, and we didn't want our customers to worry about it. And my only experience in food service was working at the Orange Julius in the mall during high school, so I thought that would worry people," Peggy said.

So the decision was made to keep the transition as quiet as possible: no newspaper advertisements, no signs, no "under new ownership" announcements. Certain loyal customers—or those who asked why Dick wasn't around as much—were told, but no fanfare was given to the move. And because Dick still made frequent visits to the store, the attempt to keep the change quiet was successful. "He would personally introduce me to as many people as possible as his son and the new owner, but that's it. It was a very gentle transition. I think we know that it was successful because people still ask, after all these years, if he still runs the place," Doug said. For Peggy, the frenzied pace of a summer night at Four Seas was still overwhelming. But having her in-laws still be part of the store, even just in the form of visits and chatting with customers, "made the transition so much smoother," she said.

It was one of Richard's tenets of good business that he be as visible and available as possible at Four Seas; management was always done on-site, which provided an opportunity for chatting with customers in between tasks. "People came to the store because they got to know the owner. They could chat with Richard at a table or watch him making the ice cream," Linda said. Over the next several years, Doug and Peggy continued the tradition of being as visible as possible at the ice cream store. Though Doug was frequently in the back making ice cream and Peggy worked a full-time job on top of the summertime work at Four Seas, both spent hours at the ice cream store in the evenings, delegating tasks and—when even the most experienced employees were overwhelmed—stepping in themselves by cleaning tables, scooping and bringing fresh three-gallon tubs of ice cream from the freezer to the fountain area.

At the same time, though he still visited to catch up with customers and the Four Seas crew, Richard and Linda became less-visible presences at the store. The move allowed Warren to move on to a new project—though not one very far removed from Four Seas. In 2006, he and author Bobbi Dempsey compiled over two hundred ice cream recipes into a book for the popular "Complete Idiot's Guide" series. The book featured favorite Four Seas flavors, as well as many other recipes Warren had compiled over the years, all reworked to be made in household ice cream makers. The book meant that for the first time Warren could share his passion for making ice cream with fans who didn't have a commercial-grade batch freezer at their disposal but who wanted to try their hands at making some of their favorite Four Seas flavors. It also gave him an opportunity to spend more time at Four Seas—it was the perfect place to hold book signings. For that summer, Richard was again a staple at Four Seas, sitting at a table in the corner or outside under a tent happily signing books, discussing the recipes and visiting with customers excited to see that the Warren family was still deeply involved with the ice cream store. "He was back in his element: talking about Four Seas with the place's best customers," Doug said.

The added time at Four Seas when he was signing books turned out to be more than just good publicity for *The Complete Idiot's Guide to Homemade Ice Cream*. For some customers, it was the last time they would ever see Richard Warren.

TRAGEDY STRIKES AGAIN

In the years after he retired from Four Seas Ice Cream, Richard Warren—now in his early seventies—kept up with the adventurous hobbies he had always enjoyed. There were rollerblading treks up and down the steep hills near the Cape Cod Canal, long mountain bike rides with his grandchildren, trips to golf courses around the country, skydiving and bungee jumping and even a memorable trip with stepchildren Michael Joyal and Jennifer Dalrymple to the top of a mountain to try heli-skiing. He traveled to France, Switzerland, Colorado and dozens of other places to test out what their famed ski resorts had to offer. The experienced skier sought out the steepest, most challenging slopes, frequently out-skiing younger friends and family members on the slopes. So the family used to his daredevil ways was shocked when they got a phone call on January 12, 2008 that, in a routine day of skiing, Richard Warren was close to death after a freak downhill skiing accident at Attitash resort, a favorite mountain in Bartlett, New Hampshire. Warren had been skiing with friends for several days when his skis hit a patch of ice and he skidded off the trail and into a large tree. A friend and former Barnstable High School teacher he'd gone skiing with nearly thirty times that year was on the mountain with him that day. Family members received calls that he was being taken off the mountain by rescuers, but before anyone could make the two-plus-hour drive, the patriarch of Four Seas had died at age seventy-two.

Four Seas owner Richard "Chief" Warren manning the ice cream machine, 2000. *Courtesy of the Warren family.*

In the intervening days, hundreds of family members, friends and Four Seas Ice Cream alumni traveled to Cape Cod to celebrate the life and mourn the death of the man known as Papa to his grandchildren and Chief to the hundreds of young people he employed and mentored in his nearly sixty years at Four Seas. Mentions appeared in dozens of local and national papers. Visiting hours held at a local funeral home drew thousands. Attendees at a funeral at the Federated Church of Hyannis, where the family had attended services for decades, spilled out onto Main Street and into extra rooms of the church, where live feeds of the funeral were broadcast. And a reception at Cummaquid Golf Club for family and friends featured stories, friends reliving comical versions of Warren's karaoke version of the Beach Boys song "Help Me Rhonda" and time for loved ones to hit one last golf ball in honor of Chief. It was an experience that still brings tears to the eyes of his friends and loved ones. Dave LeMarbre remembered:

> *It left a huge gaping hole when he passed away. A lot of history of Four Seas went away when he passed, too—the joking, the stories and the way he interacted with people is all gone. It felt like we'd lost part of the building for a while. You just can't replace him. But after the funeral and the visitation, the stuff people had to say about him was just amazing. He was a father figure to me, but he was that to a lot of people. I mean, there was never any discussion that my boys, who were in their thirties, would come to the funeral. And after, my son Michael told me that Chief was more of a grandfather figure to him than any other man in his life.*

Chief rests today in a Centerville cemetery just around the corner from Four Seas, an engraving of the iconic storefront on his gravestone. After his death, Chief became more of a presence at Four Seas than ever. On a cold January day weeks after his death, a wreath appeared on the store's door with "Hail to the Chief" emblazoned on a ribbon woven between Cape Cod hydrangeas. That summer was the first that Warren didn't welcome on opening day by giving free ice cream to the first children who came to the store that morning. But his spirit and memory didn't diminish. That July, six months after Richard Warren died, the Centerville Historical Museum on Main Street opened "Legendary: Dick Warren and Four Seas Ice Cream," an exhibit dedicated entirely to Warren and his beloved store. Culled from the museum's archives and the Warren family collection of Four Seas and ice cream memorabilia, the exhibit featured everything from old-fashioned servers' uniforms to some of Chief's more obscure collectibles. Curated by longtime Centerville resident and family friend Shirley Fisher, the exhibit was actually something Warren had hoped to organize during his life. "Three years ago I was at the ice cream shop and he said, 'With all the history in this building, why don't you do something with it?' So it was actually his idea," Fisher said in a 2008 newspaper article. Former employees, too, came together to honor Warren with a night they dubbed "We Scoop for Chief." Though they hadn't picked up ice cream scoops for several years, a group of alumni from the 1990s and 2000s joined together behind the counter to serve up ice cream to customers and remember the man who was their boss and friend. All the tips and wages the alumni earned were given to the Randall Mark Warren Scholarship Fund. They repeated the event again in 2009, testament to the fact that though years have passed, Richard Warren is still just as much a part of the business as he ever was. "People just came out of the woodwork to honor him and tell stories about him and just remember him," Doug said.

Change Comes to Four Seas

With Richard Warren's death, Four Seas Ice Cream faced one of the biggest changes in its seventy-four-year history. His presence was something customers didn't forget and commented on frequently once it was missing. But Doug and Peggy Warren also decided to embrace several positive changes, several of which Richard Warren had a hand in before his death. Aside from adding two flavors of ice cream—peanut butter chip chocolate and vanilla chai—and removing a flavor of frozen yogurt, very few changes came in the first several years of Peggy and Doug's tenure at Four Seas Ice Cream. But one that made a large impact on the profits Four Seas brought in was introducing dozens of new retail items for customers to purchase. At the time, Four Seas offered a T-shirt and several colors of baseball caps featuring the store's logo. But faced with space issues, the clothing was kept in the attic, making it difficult for employees to access and thus offer to their customers as gifts for far-flung friends or as souvenirs of their Cape Cod vacations. But next to the building, a small tent was added, allowing space for several tables' worth of merchandise to be set up daily. At first skeptical of the idea, Richard and Doug quickly grew to appreciate Peggy's choice to expand clothing offerings. After just one summer, sales took off; every year, the store now sells thousands of dollars' worth of T-shirts, hats, sweatshirts, baby items, coffee cups and other memorabilia. The new products also feature a new logo, designed and drawn by Doug. The "Cape Cod Cone" features an outline of Cape Cod in the skirt area of an ice cream cone. "It was a cool way to represent Four Seas and also the place that we love, that people associate with Four Seas," Doug said.

For years, the Warrens had received requests for ice cream to be shipped around the country to fans who wanted their beloved treat even when they couldn't make the trek to Cape Cod. The process was expensive and time-sensitive. Because of overnight shipping costs and the purchase of dry ice to keep the treat cold, shipping four quarts of ice cream could cost upward of $150. And because the dry ice only worked to keep the ice cream frozen for about two days, the customer on the receiving end needed to make sure to get the purchase into the freezer nearly immediately. Still, the concept took off, Doug said. "We've had people send quarts as get-well-soon presents, for birthdays and retirement parties and weddings." One very loyal customer in Florida even makes monthly purchases in the winter months she spends away from her Cape Cod home. Closer to home, Four Seas also began expanding in the form of pursuing wholesale accounts with local markets and restaurants. For years, Richard had kept relationships with a handful of local restaurants and markets—those that had been around nearly as long as Four Seas itself. The list was very selective. But under Doug, that practice expanded to include even more markets and several more Hyannis- and Centerville-area restaurants. One expansion also meant the beginning of custom-made flavors for specific customers. A Thai restaurant purchased ginger ice cream, an old-fashioned flavor Four Seas already served at the store. But the restaurant's owners also requested that Four Seas Ice Cream make two special flavors: green tea ice cream, made with traditional green tea powder, and red bean ice cream, an Asian delicacy that included sweet adzuki beans mixed with a basic ice cream base. Over the past several years, those custom-made flavors have included more traditional combinations, like vanilla bean and white chocolate, and stranger concoctions like those made for the Thai restaurant. Since 2010, wholesale sales have been expanded even more to include high-end markets across Cape Cod and even one about an hour away in an area of coastal Massachusetts called the South Shore. The Warrens purchased a refrigerated truck, which was never needed before, and continue to pursue selling ice cream to various markets and restaurants.

In 2009, Four Seas celebrated its seventy-fifth anniversary with a series of events throughout the summer, contests for customers and a few small changes to the store itself. The anniversary celebration kicked off in June, with two days designated "celebrity scoop days." On the first, Local Celebrity Scoop Day, members of the community—such as newspaper editors, radio talk show hosts, school officials and even the head of the local baseball league—took a turn behind the counter. On the second day, celebrities including Hollywood actors, Boston-area personalities, members of the Cape Cod Baseball League and several former Boston Bruins hockey players scooped for customers, with any tips they earned going to the Randall Mark Warren Scholarship Fund. The summer also featured a Cape Cod Ice Cream Idol ice cream contest, where customers submitted flavor ideas, which were eliminated through customer votes. At the end, the winner of the contest had her flavor made for an entire year—and that flavor, crème brûlée, became a very popular choice for many customers.

As for changes that year, customers first noticed the brightly colored T-shirts that employees wore that year, in exchange for their usual gray "crew" T-shirts. But behind the scenes, there were more changes in the works. "Our anniversary was a good opportunity to change things without people being upset about it. We could test things out and people just thought the changes were for the anniversary," Doug said. Along with a "flavor of the week," which introduced several new ice cream flavors that are still sold, the anniversary gave the Warrens an opportunity to make several small structural changes to the building and property of Four Seas itself. First came new tables to replace the aging blue Formica ones currently in place, followed by the replacement of the long fountain counter. Though seemingly small changes, several weeks of debate went into the decision to change. "At Four Seas, the tiniest changes are noticed by customers who've been coming here since they were little kids. They know the place inside and out. And if we change too much, we run the risk of alienating them," according to Doug. A change that customers embraced was the addition of a small memorial garden dedicated to Richard and Randy Warren. Marked by two granite benches bearing the two men's names, the area was also a place for customers to remember their own loved ones. For the year, Four Seas sold memorial bricks that would be engraved with whatever customers chose and then placed in the memorial garden. Money from the bricks was, of course, donated to the Randall Mark Warren Scholarship Fund, and the area now provides customers a small bit of shade and a quiet place to enjoy their summertime treats.

A New Era for Four Seas

The year 2010 marked the beginning of a new era for Four Seas, as Peggy and Doug Warren celebrated their tenth anniversary of coming to Cape Cod to begin taking over the ice cream store. Though they vowed to stay true to Richard's goals for the store—to stay a local, family-owned, old-fashioned ice cream parlor—they began pursuing their own goals to make Four Seas even more of a household name, at least on Cape Cod. The first move was to begin expanding by purchasing a second location. Several area shopping centers jumped at the idea of playing host to a second Four Seas location, but there was a problem: each of them wanted the store to stay open year-round, something that had never been done in the store's seven-decade history. With both Peggy and Doug working full-time jobs in the winter, managing a store that required them to be available year-round just wasn't an option. Then, in 2010, Doug's year-round employment came to an end when he was laid off as a teacher, and the disappointing move led him to become disillusioned with the profession and the bureaucracy surrounding it. Peggy remembers:

> He was really angry. He decided to not look at going back to teaching in another district because of it. So we looked at him going back to school, something he'd always wanted to do, and we looked at buying another store so we could finally go year-round. We just didn't think we could do it at Four Seas, thought we would need to have another place to manufacture in the winters. But we had always heard from people that if Four Seas began opening year-round, they would happily sell the ice cream wholesale. So we took another look at just winterizing Four Seas and manufacturing there. And we realized, we could get a new building and on top of purchasing it there would be another $100,000 of building costs, or we could use this one for a minimal amount of money and effort.

So in 2010, Four Seas Ice Cream celebrated its traditional closing day, the Sunday after Labor Day, with its usual sale on quarts and pints. Employees still cleaned the building from top to bottom, and they were still taken out to the annual closing day dinner to celebrate the end of another successful year. But instead of closing up the store completely, ice cream was still quietly being made in a back room for customers to purchase in quarts and pints. It was the first time in seventy-six years that customers could purchase Four Seas Ice Cream between September and May, a huge change for the store whose opening had always, for many Cape Codders, represented the unofficial beginning of summer.

By opening year-round, the Warrens could also pursue an idea they had since the beginning of their tenure at Four Seas: ice cream cakes. For several years, Peggy had experimented with ice cream pies for get-togethers with family and friends. The concoctions featured ice cream and toppings in a

Until 2010, Four Seas Ice Cream remained closed in the wintertime. *Courtesy of the Warren family.*

graham cracker piecrust and were very popular at Warren family events. But the pies were time consuming to make and between labor costs and ingredients would probably be too pricey for customers to choose them for their own gatherings, the Warrens decided. The next version of what would become the Four Seas Ice Cream cake was Doug's "cake in a quart," which featured layered chocolate and vanilla ice cream sandwiching the store's famous homemade hot fudge and chocolate cookie crumbles. Again, they were popular at family get-togethers. But the "quart cakes" were difficult to slice and serve, so once again the idea was tabled.

Finally, the first ice cream cake was created in the winter of 2010, just in time for Thanksgiving. Like the quart cake, it featured chocolate ice cream, then a layer of hot fudge and cookie crumbles, then a layer of vanilla ice cream, topped with a whipped cream frosting and decorated by hand to reflect the holiday or event a customer was celebrating. The treat took off immediately and continues to grow in popularity. In November 2011, just 35 cakes were sold. By December, when holiday-themed cakes went on sale along with a new ice cream combination of chocolate and peppermint stick, 90 cakes were sold. Following the popularity of those two holiday-themed cakes, Valentine's Day and Easter cakes were also sold. By the summer of 2011, the cakes were a bona fide success. "In August alone, we sold 125 cakes. The word of mouth was amazing, the news had spread. We actually had people buying a cake for every single holiday and birthday party. They were hooked. We now do 20 to 25 cakes per week. We're actually running out of room for them and are contemplating building more freezer space just for the cakes," Doug said. The success of the cakes has led the Warrens to consider expanding to

Starting in 2010, Four Seas began making ice cream cakes for holidays, birthdays and celebrations. *Photo by the author.*

include even more ice cream novelties, such as Peggy's ice cream pies and even chocolate-covered ice cream bars.

Opening year-round has also allowed the Warrens to expand their business to multiple locations—without purchasing a second location. In 2011, the couple again considered purchasing a second location for the store. This time, the owner of a local ice cream store just a few towns over had chosen to retire and was offering his twenty-five-year-old business for sale. The Warrens were one of several groups in the running to take over the business but eventually decided it just wasn't the best move for Four Seas. "We already had name recognition. We didn't need their name recognition, and they were charging for it. So we decided it wasn't the right move for us financially, and we backed away," Peggy said. For decades, Richard Warren had instilled the idea that opening a second location might bring additional revenue and introduce Four Seas to a new group of customers in an entirely different location, but there were also pitfalls with that plan. He had seen them in other ice cream businesses, both through his work with Successful Ice Cream Retailing and at local and national ice cream retailers' association conferences. "He knew retailers who opened a second or a third location and it caused the whole establishment to die. He made a good living and had a nice life. Why ruin that? And I've tried to keep the same focus as my dad, to do one thing and do it well. Why be greedy?" Doug said.

Instead, the Warrens chose to begin selling their ice cream to a few selected stores for scooping, not just in pints and quarts. The practice had been done before, when tubs of ice cream were sold to coffee shops or cafés, but some business owners would get frustrated that they couldn't sell the same kind of ice cream to customers year-round and were forced to switch to a different product once the winter rolled around. With Doug Warren now producing ice cream every month of the year, several retailers decided to try again, with two—one in the village of Hyannis, right next door to Centerville, and one a few towns away in Sandwich. On Main Street in Hyannis, a sign advertised that the shop was scooping Four Seas ice cream, and the store quickly became competition for the ice cream store that had always operated across the street. "Doing this basically allowed us the visibility of opening another store without the overhead of paying employees, overhead or a mortgage. It's a good fit for us at this point," Doug said.

Changing, but Still the Same

Operating year-round opened Four Seas Ice Cream to a completely new revenue stream and allowed loyal customers to purchase their favorite ice cream in the wintertime, as well as try new products such as ice cream cakes that the Warrens don't have time to experiment with in the summertime when Four Seas' business season is in full swing. But despite the changes, one experience reminds Doug that changing or expanding too much would actually be detrimental to Four Seas and would likely disappoint many of its customers:

> A couple of years ago, I was going to change all the hand-painted signs and hand-written prices on the walls at Four Seas. They're the same posters from decades ago. We just mark out the prices and put new ones as the years go on. Or my dad would cut the letters off the old poster boards and just glue them to new posters. So I was going to have new signs professionally made, just to make things look a little more polished. But literally on the same day I was going to order the signs, an older woman came into the store and I overheard her telling a friend she'd been coming to the store since she was a child, then brought her children and now her grandchildren. And the one thing she told her friend she hoped never changed? "The hokey signs," she said. She told her friend she loved that they never changed, even if they are tacky. She joked that in the time she'd been coming to Four Seas, only the

Loyal customers enjoying lunch at Four Seas. *Courtesy of the Warren family.*

A couple of Four Seas favorites—a chocolate chip cookie ice cream sandwich and a quart of ice cream. *Photo by the author.*

A Continuing Family Legacy

A typical busy day at Four Seas. Owners Peggy (in background) and Douglas (in foreground) spent time behind the counter helping customers and employees. *Courtesy of the* Barnstable Patriot.

> *Coca-Cola machine changed every ten years. And it made me realize, people like that homemade, sort of tacky look. Everyone wants to be this sort of modern place, like a Starbucks. But with Four Seas, you've got this one place that never changes. It's so romantic to come back and be transported to your childhood. I haven't changed a single sign since. I laminated a couple of them, but that's it.*

In that vein, though the Warrens have considered expanding to a second location somewhere else on Cape Cod, they have resisted being spread too thin. Both Richard and Linda Warren and Peggy and Doug Warren have turned down offers to discuss putting Four Seas Ice Cream into major chain supermarkets, choosing instead to stock only in small, locally owned shops in the area. Rather than selling ice cream to every restaurant possible, they instead only pick shops with similar feelings about bringing good-quality food to Cape Cod. And though several offers of financial backing to expand to a small chain have been made, the Warrens have chosen to keep Four Seas what it has always been: a small, family-owned business. Peggy said:

> *People come to Four Seas because it's Four Seas, not some chain. Customers want to see the owners working at the business. That's what America was built on, people who are really hands-on with their*

A family celebrating the Fourth of July at Four Seas Ice Cream, date unknown. *Courtesy of the Warren family.*

businesses. Not these big conglomerates. We don't want to be the next Ben & Jerry's. If we're managing a bunch of franchises from an office somewhere, that's not what our customers would want. I truly believe you can't call it a family-owned business unless it's a family-run business, too.

A Continuing Family Legacy

In the next several years, as the popularity of Four Seas as a winter treat as well as a summer destination grows, the Warrens haven't ruled out the possibility of eventually expanding to that oft-talked-about second location. It's a dream, too, that in the future both of the Warrens' children could become involved in the business, and having two locations would make that more feasible. A second location would only be considered, however, if a family member is running it, Peggy said; a tenet that all members of the Warren family agree would be necessary to even consider expanding. Linda believes it's the family atmosphere that has kept customers returning year after year, sometimes making hours-long trips just for a taste of ice cream. "They come because it's good ice cream but also because their parents did it, and their parents' parents did it. And it's happy. You might see a crab in an ice cream store, but it's very rare," she said.

There have been changes at Four Seas over its nearly eighty years in operation, including new flavors, new uniforms for employees and new spruce-ups to keep the aging building in the best shape possible. But the dedication to keeping the store in the family hasn't waned—and if the Warren family has anything to do with it, it never will. Jennifer Dalrymple, daughter of Linda and Richard Warren, said it's that dedication that ensures her that her two young children, still just toddlers, will have a place at Four Seas someday. "They know that it's their Uncle Doug and Aunt Peggy that run it and their Papa before that. Every time we drive by, they notice Uncle Doug's truck there. What makes this place special to my kids is that they know it's going to be a part of their lives. At least I hope it will be."

Chapter 5
FAMOUS FANS OF FOUR SEAS

In 1986, during a hot, sunny week in the middle of one of the busiest tourist months on Cape Cod, the beaches, hotels and roads were more packed than usual. National media outlets clambered to get near the home where a giant tent was being set up, guarded by security guards at all edges of the property. Photos were clandestinely taken over fences, from boats and through trees. Questions were asked of next-door neighbors, florists and caterers. And all eyes were on the villages of Centerville and next-door Hyannisport as Caroline Kennedy prepared to wed.

The daughter of late president John F. Kennedy and Jacqueline Kennedy, then Onassis, brought hundreds of well-wishers and reporters to the usually quiet beachside area of Hyannisport, just a couple miles down the road from Centerville. They lined South Main Street in Centerville from Our Lady of Victory Catholic Church, past Four Seas and down Craigville Beach Road, into Hyannisport, where the famed Kennedy Compound is still located. Speculation about Caroline Kennedy's wedding filtered through homes and shops in the area, and news reports appeared almost daily guessing what the dinner, the dress and the party would be like. While speculation reached a crescendo on the eve of the wedding, the Kennedys were enjoying some of their favorite Cape Cod staples— including Four Seas Ice Cream.

Four Seas came into the national spotlight at that time, ending up in news outlets across the United States whose representatives had come out for the first daughter's sumptuous marriage to Edwin Schlossberg, a New

York entrepreneur and artist. On July 18, 1986, *USA Today* wrote, "The lawn of the Kennedy compound here has sprouted a gleaning white tent, where 400 guests will dine and dance after the ceremony. New York decorators are transforming the Hyannisport Country Club for tonight's gala rehearsal dinner. The Kennedys' favorite ice cream shop is delivering vats of peach—Jackie and Caroline's favorite."

Caroline Kennedy's attempts to keep her life—and her wedding—private were the stuff of legends, so when tidbits about her favorite sweet came to light, it made headlines. But the truth is, one of the country's most famous political families has been intertwined with Four Seas for generations. The Kennedy clan's connection to the Cape began before Four Seas was open. John F. "Honey Fitz" Fitzgerald, a mayor of Boston and United States representative, spent time in Falmouth Heights. But when it was time to find a family vacation spot, son-in-law Joseph Kennedy, who married Fitzgerald's daughter Rose, turned to Hyannisport, a small town with no stop lights, a tiny post office and few commercial enterprises save a newspaper stand. Its homes, mostly seasonal, are a combination of the small cottages typical of Cape Cod and stately mansions used by some of the country's wealthiest residents as escapes from the daily grind.

A church modeled on St. Anthony's of Scotland and a golf course reminiscent of that storied establishment overlook a glittering ocean. Hyannisport's streets are narrow and winding, often closed in on both sides by beach grass. Sand spills into roadways. In 1925, Joseph Kennedy rented a home in Hyannisport and three years later bought the property, securing the Cape as a Kennedy destination for nearly one hundred years. In the summer of 1960, over twenty-five years before his daughter was to marry in Centerville, all eyes were on the area as the newly elected John Fitzgerald Kennedy accepted his nomination as president of the United States at the National Guard Armory in Hyannis.

Over the years, the family's property holdings expanded to include a number of large homes on the water where various members of the family brought their children for summers of sailing, playing golf, swimming—and eating Four Seas Ice Cream. Members of the Kennedy family were the only customers who were allowed to have a charge account at the ice cream store, Dick Warren said in an interview in 1980. "Warren says he has extended a few special privileges to the Kennedys over the years. Many celebrities have been known to frequent his store, but Warren says he maintains a charge account for the Kennedys alone."

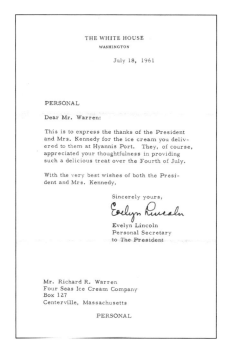

THE WHITE HOUSE
WASHINGTON

July 18, 1961

PERSONAL

Dear Mr. Warren:

This is to express the thanks of the President and Mrs. Kennedy for the ice cream you delivered to them at Hyannis Port. They, of course, appreciated your thoughtfulness in providing such a delicious treat over the Fourth of July.

With the very best wishes of both the President and Mrs. Kennedy,

Sincerely yours,

Evelyn Lincoln

Evelyn Lincoln
Personal Secretary
to The President

Mr. Richard R. Warren
Four Seas Ice Cream Company
Box 127
Centerville, Massachusetts

PERSONAL

A letter from the White House to Richard Warren from President John F. Kennedy. *Courtesy of the Warren family.*

"They come in here after tennis or the beach and they charge cones. They never carry any money," he said. Douglas Warren also remembers seeing the Kennedys when he was a young child, he said. The Kennedys also received special treatment in the form of delivery. On multiple occasions, Dick himself brought tubs of ice cream to the Hyannisport Kennedy Compound, as it came to be known.

A staunch Republican, Warren may not have agreed with the family's politics, but he wasn't above helping out a good customer. "I don't usually deliver. I'm a busy man. But for the president of the United States, what the hell, I'll deliver," he told the *Boston Herald*. One of the most famous deliveries was brought to the Hyannisport Club in July 1986, when John F. Kennedy's daughter, Caroline Kennedy, was to wed her longtime beau. According to the *Patriot Ledger* newspaper:

> When Jacqueline Kennedy Onassis insisted on serving her favorite Four Seas homemade peach ice cream at her daughter's prenuptial dinner yesterday, ice cream maker Dick Warren was hardly surprised. "The Kennedys have been coming here for three generations," Warren said. His small shop, Cape Cod's oldest homemade ice cream establishment, is located a few hundred yards from Our Lady of Victory Church, where Caroline Kennedy is set to marry artist-entrepreneur Edwin Schlossberg today. Onassis made a special request for Four Seas peach for the 100-guest rehearsal dinner at the Hyannis Port Club and told waiters to serve it with fresh peaches and blueberries."

Above all, Four Seas' fresh peach ice cream, made only for a few weeks in July and August when Georgia peaches are in season, was what brought the family to Centerville—though not necessarily into the store. Jacqueline

Kennedy used to visit the store but often didn't get out of the chauffeured limousine that brought her there, Doug remembers. "She would pull up out front in her limo, a Secret Service agent would come in and grab her ice cream and he would hand it to her through the window," he said. "And she always had her stereotypical big old glasses on."

Sometimes, those glasses caused even employees to not recognize "Jackie O." when she visited the store. "This lady comes in and she's got these big sunglasses, shorts and a sleeveless shirt. She looked completely normal. I didn't even look at her and asked to help her. She ordered fresh peach, gave me the money and left. I didn't think anything of it. But I turned around and went into the back room, and Chief is just there dying laughing, when he tells me who I just served. I had no idea. She had totally disguised herself," Trish LeMarbre, a former employee, said. Another time, Dick himself had to open a tab for $2.50 for the famous presidential spouse because both she and her Secret Service bodyguards had forgotten their wallets and didn't have enough pocket change to cover a couple of cones. "They were short fifteen cents," he told the *Patriot Ledger* newspaper.

In recent years, Ethel Kennedy, widow of Robert F. Kennedy, has started a new tradition in the form of a new flavor. For the past few years, very early in the season she has called the store to order its classic mocha chip ice cream—but without the chocolate chips. "We make her almost forty quarts and she buys the whole batch," Doug said. The quarts are kept in the store's freezer until Ethel or a member of her staff comes to pick them up. By the end of the summer, all of the mocha-without-chips quarts are gone, headed back to Ethel's Hyannisport home.

A check for six dollars from President John F. Kennedy, and the envelope it was sent in from the White House, that the president sent to Four Seas Ice Cream in 1962. *Courtesy of the Warren family.*

Sometimes, visits to Four Seas from the Kennedys had a surprising effect on customers. Linda Warren remembers one of Dick's favorite stories to tell, about the time President John F. Kennedy, known as Jack, came in with his friend Roosevelt "Rosey" Grier, a professional football player:

> *Jackie Kennedy and Rosey Grier came in frequently. One day they came in and there was a woman in the store who came in just before them and got a cone. She was just getting ready to leave when Jackie and Rosey walked in ready to order. She notices that it's Jackie Kennedy. And Richard told me he saw her go out the door, throw her cone into the garbage can and come inside just to stand beside Jack and Rosey.*

"He was a humongous person," Doug said of Grier. "As a little kid, I could have sworn he took up two stools out front."

Another woman who came in at the same time as the then-president had a similarly shocked reaction, Doug remembered. When the woman saw him, she put the ice cream cone in her hand into her purse rather than the keys she was holding in the other palm.

Legendary United States senator Edward "Ted" Kennedy was another staunch supporter of the store, Doug said. In 1994, Ted Kennedy sent a letter to Dick Warren congratulating him on the store's longevity:

> *Dear Dick: I am delighted to offer my warm personal congratulations and best wishes to all of you on the sixtieth anniversary of the Four Seas. I'd also like to congratulate you, Dick, on your thirty-eighth anniversary as the owner of this greatly enjoyed part of the Centerville community. I know personally that I and all of the Kennedys have loved going to the Four Seas over the years and we certainly look forward to your continued success.*

Until his death in 2009, Ted Kennedy was a frequent visitor to Four Seas and even wrote about his love for the sweet treat in his 2008 biography, *True Compass*. After being diagnosed with a brain tumor, Kennedy writes, he decided to dedicate the summer to his family, love of sailing and desire for the family's favorite ice cream. "I decided that I was finally going to indulge my passion for Four Seas, the legendary ice cream that is freshly made on Cape Cod only in the summer. I may be the only patient in the history of Massachusetts General who went through both chemotherapy and radiation and gained weight!"

Other Kennedys who frequent the store have included Robert Kennedy Jr., son of the late Robert F. Kennedy and an activist and attorney. Maria Shriver, the daughter of Eunice Kennedy Shriver, frequently visited with her children and then-husband Arnold Schwarzenegger. Schwarzenegger, at the time the governor of California, once visited the store at 10:30 p.m. right as it closed for the store's once-a-month cleaning. As members of the staff worked around him, moving boxes and scrubbing floors, he happily chatted and answered questions.

OTHER CELEBRITY ENCOUNTERS

Though members of the Kennedy family have been some of the most staunchly loyal celebrity fans of Four Seas, the store has been visited by dozens of other famous ice cream lovers over the years. Many of them have homes on Cape Cod or the islands of Nantucket or Martha's Vineyard, which are a short ferry ride away.

But like the thousands of other tourists who visit Cape Cod every summer, other celebrities are called to the Cape for its beaches, perfect summer weather and relaxing atmosphere. For many Four Seas employees under Dick Warren in the late 1970s, a series of visits by legendary comic Bob Hope and his wife, Delores, was a highlight. Douglas Warren, who was in high school and working at the store on those nights, said the couple came in for six consecutive nights while Bob performed comedy shows at the local entertainment venue the Cape Cod Melody Tent in Hyannis. The couple would drive the few miles from the Melody Tent, which each summer hosts comedians and musicians in an open-air venue, to Four Seas Ice Cream in a limousine, Doug said. They would usually arrive around the time the store closed "so they could come in here and nobody could harass them," Doug said. He remembered, "Bob was a vanilla person. He'd usually chat for about ten minutes and then go out to the limo and fall asleep. And Delores would stay for the full half hour as we closed up the shop. She was just a delight to talk to, and she just loved finding out all about us."

The couple only visited the store one summer, but those six visits had an impact on the famous comedian, Doug said. At his final show before moving on, Hope joked that it was a good thing he was leaving because, since visiting Four Seas every night, he was having trouble climbing onto the stool placed on the stage for him during his comedy sets.

Comedian and actor Eddie Murphy visited the store at the height of his fame in the 1990s, Doug said, adding that the experience was a unique one. "He had a bodyguard taste the ice cream before he would eat it," Doug remembered.

Though not a comedian by trade, Steven Tyler, singer for the rock band Aerosmith and a judge on the popular *American Idol* television show, made a comical impression on one Four Seas employee. Tyler and the band's bassist, Tom Hamilton, are regulars at Four Seas and own homes in the area. But once, employee Alison Taylor Serpico, who worked at the store in the early 2000s, encountered Steven Tyler in an unexpected place.

I was scooping ice cream up front and everyone was saying that Steve Tyler was at table seven eating a banana split. I just remember the whole thing sounded like a big joke. Regardless, I decided to walk past his table and went into the sandwich room and started washing my hands. He came in and asked where he could wash his hands, and I said he could either do it in the boys' room or with me. So we washed our hands, and when I asked him why he was on Cape Cod, he said he was there to see me.

The ice cream had a similarly positive affect on one of modern comedy's brightest stars: Adam Sandler. Filming a movie, *That's My Boy*, in Osterville in the summer of 2011, Sandler and other members of the film's cast and crew became equally addicted to a daily fix of Four Seas Ice Cream. The love started when the crew was looking for a recommendation for ice cream places in the area, Doug said. The father of a Four Seas Ice Cream employee was doing security for the set in his capacity as a Barnstable police officer and suggested Four Seas. A few minutes later, Warren said, he received a call asking if he could bring ice cream to the set. He did—and got the call several more times over the course of shooting. When a friend from high school working on the set announced who he was, "all these people started clapping for me. I sort of felt like a celebrity myself," he said.

Ross Gabrielli, co-owner of Gala Catering, which handled all the food for the film, said Four Seas Ice Cream—especially the most popular flavor, butter crunch—became nearly essential to the cast and crew:

The whole cast and crew would get excited when they found out the ice cream was from Four Seas. One day we were filming far from Four Seas and had to use another company for our ice cream. Let's just say the crew was upset at me for not coming through, even for only one day. Every day we had requests for Four Seas, from extras and producers and Sandler himself.

The comedian, famous for a host of blockbuster comedy films, was such a fan that he visited the store several times on his own, Doug said. Sandler, like Hope, visited the store right as it closed for chest cleaning, meaning there were no customers but the entire staff was on hand. "But he was just very, very friendly," Warren said. "Even as I was trying to get kids to work instead of gawk at him."

Sandler also visited the store on two other occasions, once on a date with his wife and a second time to purchase frappes and Four Seas Ice Cream T-shirts for the whole family, Doug said. Though he was asked for autographs by dozens of customers, the Four Seas Ice Cream policy about employees not doing so was followed. And that's one of the reasons why celebrities keep coming back to the store, Warren believes.

Since Four Seas Ice Cream became famous in its early decades of operation, the owners have kept the same policy of treating celebrities like any other customers, Linda Warren said. "One of the things we always told the kids was, 'Just leave them alone.' No autographs, no nothing. They're here to buy ice cream just like everybody else." Douglas has continued the tradition, and employees still are not allowed to ask for autographs—though some of them try to sneak one when owners and managers aren't looking. "I'm sort of like my dad in that respect, I guess. I try not to stare at them, try not to treat them any differently than anyone else," he said. Four Seas also isn't like many other places that attract celebrities. On the walls are photos of customers, old news clippings and staff members but no pictures of famous patrons— something Doug says won't change anytime soon.

In New England, this treat—known as a milkshake in most areas of the United States—is called a frappe. *Photo by the author.*

Our philosophy over the years has been to just treat them like people. Our employees can't take pictures or autographs, and we've never put a photo of any celebrity on the wall. And it's cool because they seem to feel comfortable coming in here. I'm sure some of them get their egos stroked by having their picture on the wall, but others just want to be left alone to have something that's good quality. And they know they're not going to get harassed.

Four Seas has also attracted dozens of other celebrities, including:

TELEVISION PERSONALITIES: Katie Couric, Bob Villa, Gene Rayburn, David Hartman

MUSICIANS: James Taylor, Carly Simon, John Denver, members of the band Little Feat

ACTORS: Ryan Reynolds, Susan Sarandon, Tim Robbins, Eva Amurri, Cheryl Hines, Blake Lively, Neal McDonough, Anne Heche, Paul Guilfoyle, Bill Daily, Marie Osmond, Michael Ian Black, Scott Wolf

ATHLETES: Boston Celtics legend Larry Bird, professional hockey player Dan LaCouture, Olympic figure skater and coach Paul Wylie

Chapter 6
HOW THE FAMOUS ICE CREAM IS MADE

Early in the morning, before the hot summer sun has attracted thousands of tourists to nearby Craigville Beach, Four Seas Ice Cream owner Douglas Warren hunches over the marble countertop to begin calculating how much ice cream will need to be made for the coming day. The sun comes up over the hill Four Seas sits on, revealing empty streets still wet with dew and, maybe, the occasional dog walker or biker getting in their morning exercise before the heat and the visitors it attracts take over the sidewalks. A cup of steaming black coffee in one hand and a pencil in the other, Warren pores over water-warped pages from the same day exactly one year earlier. The pages list the amounts of ice cream made, how busy the store was, whether the sun was up or it was raining or humid or unseasonably chilly.

It is 4:30 a.m.

Periodically, he makes notations on a similar but blank page, finally deciding how many batches of each flavor of homemade ice cream will need to be made. The page is filled with notations of how many quarts, pints and three-gallon tubs will need to be filled in order to keep up with the crowds that flow into Four Seas between 9:00 a.m. and 10:30 p.m. every day. An hour later, or maybe an hour and a half, the employee who will serve as ice cream maker for the day, usually an experienced employee who has worked at the store for several summers, arrives. He enters the cooler to pull out the cream, flavorings, fruits and nuts that, over the course of several hours, will be turned into Four Seas' famous ice creams.

The same scene plays out four days per week every summer, the same way it has for nearly eighty years. Before Doug, his father, Richard, sat at the same line of blue stools calculating ice cream freezes over breakfast, his characteristic white pants and apron still pristine. But not for long, because around 6:30 a.m. the ice cream making begins, a slow churning from the machine the only noise coming from the store.

The time-honored tradition of a member of the Warren family sitting at the counter early in the morning is only one small part of the Four Seas Ice Cream tradition of making their signature sweet treat. Even before Dick Warren began working at the store, before he took over and far before Douglas Warren purchased the business in the 2000s, W. Wells Watson was using a very similar method to prepare the ice cream.

Old-Fashioned Freezers

Since its beginning, Four Seas Ice Cream has used a type of ice cream maker called a batch freezer, an old-fashioned type of freezer that most ice cream stores stopped using in the middle of the twentieth century. After World War II, when clever engineering allowed freezer technology to grow in leaps and bounds, most stores chose to use an easier method of making ice cream called continuous freezing. Continuous freezers use pipes to constantly pump ice cream ingredients and flavorings into a freezer compartment, so only one flavor can be made in large quantities at any given time. "That day you're just making all vanilla or all chocolate," Doug said. "The whole process is different and not really conducive to putting in fresh fruits or other ingredients."

Before commercial freezers came along, though, there were a host of other types of ice cream makers that required more work but allowed ice cream manufacturers to take a very hands-on approach to their product. Historically speaking, ice cream was long considered an extravagance enjoyed by the wealthy because of the time and effort involved in making the treat. It was first enjoyed in America during the colonial days after migrating over from England and France beginning in the seventeenth century, maybe even in the colonial villages on Cape Cod.

Paving the way for stores like Four Seas, an ice cream store on a road called Chatham Street in New York City was identified as the very first ice cream shop back in the late 1700s. Coincidentally, Chatham is also the name of a town on Cape Cod just a little over a half hour from the village of

Centerville. Even then, despite its price, ice cream was a popular indulgence. In 1790, President George Washington spent around $200 for ice cream at that Chatham Street store.

In the 1840s, Nancy Johnson of Philadelphia invented a paddle-operated ice cream maker that eliminated the hand churning previously required. It was the predecessor of the type of freezers that Four Seas and other stores use.

Four Seas Ice Cream's batch freezers aren't quite as complicated and certainly allow everyone, not just the wealthy, to enjoy their creations. According to Doug, Four Seas has always used batch freezers made by Emery Thompson, a company that patented that type of freezer in 1906. (It was a lucky time to invent such a creation, since just two years earlier at the St. Louis World Exposition, as rumor goes, the first waffle cones were invented.) Emery Thompson's first models of batch freezers were simply cylinder containers encased by a slightly larger cylindrical container on a pair of legs. The inner cylinder contained two turning blades that would scrape the ice cream off the sides of the cylinder, mixing that frozen ice cream with the still-liquid ice cream churning away. Between the inner and outer cylinders was room for freezing gas, which would act as the agent to cool the ice cream inside the inner cylinder.

At one end was an opening for ingredients to be added and at the other a slot with a cover where the finished product would be propelled out of the machine. Once the ice cream had churned long enough for all of it to reach a semi-frozen state, the ice cream would flow out of the slot, according to Emery Thompson's patent for its first ice cream batch freezer. An ice cream maker could create a semi-continuous freezing state by taking out the ice cream from one batch and immediately adding the ingredients for the next batch without the need to turn the machine on and off repeatedly, the patent stated.

In Four Seas' early years, the Emery Thompson machine used by W. Wells Watson had a twenty-quart capacity, about half the size of the freezers currently used at the store. The machine had a similar design to Emery Thompson's original 1906 freezer. But after Four Seas' notoriety spread across the Cape and the store became busy nearly every day, the twenty-quart machine just couldn't keep up with business, Doug said. So one of the first things Richard Warren did after purchasing the business in 1960 was replace the twenty-quart freezer with one that could produce forty quarts with each batch of ice cream. Doug remembers:

Chief didn't like the fact that when he was working for Watson he'd sometimes run out of ice cream on a Saturday night or a Sunday night, which is kind of prime time for the store. He didn't really want to run the ice cream machine twenty-four/seven, which is basically what he would have needed in order to keep up with the growing demand. So in the first couple of years, he put in one that could do twice the volume in basically the same footprint, without taking up any more space in the ice cream making room.

That machine was used to churn out all of Four Seas' ice creams for the next twenty years, until in 1980, a midsummer malfunction meant it had to be taken out of use and a new one purchased. "We had to go out and spend $40,000 on this machine in the middle of the summer," said Doug, who was in high school at the time of the purchase. "But we had to because you can't exactly sell ice cream without the ice cream maker."

The older machine sat in the Warrens' basement for two years before a refrigeration expert fixed it up. It was sold to an ice cream store proprietor in Canada, Doug remembered—and it's still going strong making ice cream today.

The ice cream maker purchased for Four Seas in 1980 is still being used to churn out every ounce of the store's product—nearly two thousand gallons per week during most of the seventeen weeks of "peak season."

Making the Product

Doug Warren and one other employee spend four days per week making ice cream, usually about fifty "freezes" per day of approximately ten gallons each. Each morning begins with about an hour of "figuring" the freeze—deciding how many gallons of each flavor are needed so that the store doesn't run out the next day. Ice cream is usually made a couple of days ahead. For example, most of the ice cream made on Tuesday will stay in the freezer until Thursday or Friday, when stocks from earlier in the week have been depleted by several days of visits.

While Doug finishes up calculating the amount of ice cream that will be made, the ice cream maker begins getting ingredients ready for the first few freezes. Ice cream mix—a combination of cream, milk and a stabilizer—is brought from the cooler into the ice cream making room, a cramped space that also contains freezers for quarts and pints. Each day, the different

How the Famous Ice Cream Is Made

An employee uses a "milk bomb" to pour ice cream mix into Four Seas' single-batch ice cream maker. *Photo by Jennifer Badalamenti/Roots Workshop.*

flavors of ice cream are made in the same order to avoid contamination by different colorings, flavorings and, for allergy reasons, ingredients such as nuts and peanut butter.

The ice cream maker adds about five gallons of ice cream mix and whips it into nine to ten gallons of ice cream. That represents an overrun of about 50 percent, about half of what many ice cream stores use, Doug said. "You can get as much as twelve gallons of ice cream out of five gallons of mix, but we don't. And we don't want to."

The mix used at Four Seas is also different from many stores because of its butterfat content. Butterfat, the fatty part of milk and cream, "is what gives the body of the ice cream, the mouthfeel," Doug said. It is measured in percentages of the total amount of liquid. For example, one percent milk contains one percent of its total weight in fat. Soft serve, known by ice cream makers as "ice milk," contains less than ten percent butterfat. That means it contains less fat but won't be as decadent or creamy as its higher-butterfat counterparts. Ice cream is considered to have between ten and sixteen percent butterfat. At Four Seas, mix with a fifteen percent butterfat is used because of its perfect combination of creaminess and mellow flavor, Doug said. Deciding on fifteen percent butterfat was a process that included, over the years, tasting ice cream mixes with many different butterfats from several different companies.

"I've tried a lot of sixteen percent butterfats. Often, the sixteen percent butterfats are cooked at a higher temperature for pasteurization than the lower butterfats. It means they have a longer shelf life, but I just don't like the flavor. Cooking gives it a different flavor," he said. Another type of ice cream, known as "super premium," contains seventeen percent or above butterfat. But Doug thinks the flavor of the cream often comes through rather than the ingredients in the ice cream, meaning it isn't the best choice for delicate flavors like ginger, fresh peach or cantaloupe. He said:

> I haven't tasted anything above a sixteen percent that's worthy of putting into our ice cream. It becomes just too creamy and you can't taste the ingredients. Or you have to spend a lot of money to get the ice cream to taste how you want it to. It's kind of counterproductive, and most people can't really discern the difference about sixteen percent anyway.

After ice cream mix is added to the freezer, the flavorings follow. For vanilla, it's that simple: a 100 percent pure vanilla extract is added to the ice cream. Other flavors that don't contain candies, nuts, chocolate or fruits have additional flavorings added. For example, a rum and butter ice cream has real rum added to it, Doug said. Caramel cream ice cream has a steady stream of caramel added to the ice cream maker as it churns the vanilla-based ice cream. And coffee ice cream contains coffee syrup, a traditional New England flavoring that's often mixed with milk to create a sweet breakfast drink. Chocolate is made with a rich mix of several chocolate syrups and real chocolate.

After the liquid flavorings are added, a switch is turned to begin the refrigeration process of the ice cream. Just like in Emery Thompson's original 1906 ice cream batch freezer, an outside metal cylinder fills with a coolant, which brings the internal cylinder and the cream inside it to a lower temperature. It takes about seven minutes for the refrigerated cream to drop from about thirty-four degrees Fahrenheit to twenty degrees below zero, Doug said. "That's when it starts to get really thick, and the two metal scrapers inside scrape the ice cream off the cool sides of the cylinder until it reaches the correct consistency."

It takes between seven and ten minutes for the batch of ice cream to be complete, he said. The ice cream that comes out of the machine isn't the

Four Seas Ice Cream owner Douglas Warren makes ice cream with his son, Joshua. *Photo by the author.*

consistency it is when it's scooped onto a cone or into a sundae. It comes out at a soft-serve-like consistency, smooth enough to go directly from the machine into quart and pint containers, called pre-packing. The rest is put into old-fashioned metal cans—"so we're not wasting paper or plastic," Doug says—that will be used in the fountain area.

It's important not to keep the ice cream in the freezer too long in order to make sure that the texture is exactly the same way it has been for Four Seas' long history. The longer the ice cream is in the machine, the more rotating it does in the internal cylinder and the more air is whipped into it, Doug said. "At some point we shut down the refrigeration. You don't want to leave the ice cream sitting too long or the machine will whip air into it and make it light and fluffy. Too light and fluffy for us. We want it to be a bit more dense."

Sometimes, during very long freezes, the ice cream is transferred to a large crank-operated funnel, which holds the ice cream as it's slowly, manually pumped into quarts and pints. It's usually used when freezes are nearly or completely made up of pints and quarts, with no extra ice cream to go into metal cans for scooping. While most of the flavors can go through the funnel, certain ones are avoided, such as chocolate chip cookie dough and chip chocolate, because of the large chunks of cookie dough and chocolate.

Four Seas offers twenty-four of its thirty-four flavors on the menu for scooping. All flavors are always available in pints and quarts. In the spring, when ice cream purchases are much lower than in the months of June, July and August, around 70 percent of the flavors are made on any given day. In the middle of the summer, there are times when every single flavor is made in the course of a single day of ice-cream making. Those days can sometimes last up to twelve hours, Doug said, with the longest ice cream making day on record at Four Seas lasting fourteen hours. Doug averages around forty-five hours per week just making ice cream, he said. The most ice cream ever made in a single day was sixty-five batches, or about 150 gallons of ice cream.

Four Seas adheres to a strict routine of which ice creams are made when, Doug said, in order to avoid contamination. Vanilla is always made first. Then usually is coffee, which is simply vanilla ice cream with an additional flavor added. Then it's on to chocolate ice cream, the rich flavor of which will drown out any residual coffee flavors. That's followed by mocha chip, a mixture of chocolate and coffee ice creams with two types of chocolate chips, made since "it's a natural progression from coffee," Doug said. Between every few flavors, the ice cream machine is cleaned out to make sure each group of flavors doesn't bleed into the next.

How the Famous Ice Cream Is Made

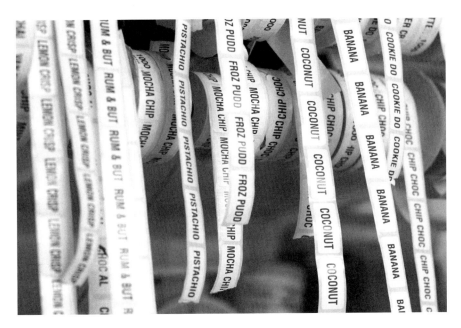

Stickers with the names of flavors are hand placed onto every quart of ice cream that Four Seas sells. *Photo by Jennifer Badalamenti/Roots Workshop.*

The process begins again with lighter-colored flavors such as chocolate chip cookie dough, mint chocolate chip (pink because of its peppermint flavoring) and chip chocolate, a vanilla-based ice cream with Four Seas' unique twist on chocolate chips. Fruit flavors are usually grouped together, Doug said, and then the sherbets and sorbets. Peanut butter chocolate chip is always made last in the machine so that people with severe nut allergies can feel safe eating flavors that were made hours before with several thorough washings of the ice cream freezer in between.

Sherbets and sorbets are made slightly differently than ice creams, Doug said. Sherbets are a mixture of cream and water with fruit juices, extracts and flavorings. Usually, about a third of their volume comes from cream, with the rest from water, sugar and fruit. Sorbets contain no dairy whatsoever and are made of water, sugar, fruit and flavorings. The process of making sherbets and sorbets begins at least twelve hours before the batch of fruit-based frozen dessert is scheduled to be made the next day. In giant five-gallon milk jugs called "milk bombs," water, flavorings, fruits and a stabilizer, usually corn syrup, are mixed together. For sherbets, a small amount of cream is also added. The mixtures sit overnight so the ingredients become mixed well, Doug said. For decades, Four Seas has offered a traditional Cape Cod cranberry sherbet and a popular orange flavor. Lemon sorbet, which tastes a lot like the lemonade that is added to it, has also been made for a long time, Doug said. "When I was a kid, I remember, we didn't make any sorbets. We had lemon sherbet and lime sherbet, which we don't have anymore, along with our orange and cranberry." The flavors are popular on very hot summer days when a decadent flavor just wouldn't be as refreshing, he said. Because the flavors are water-based, they take just a little longer in the ice cream freezer before they are added to quarts and pints. Though sherbets and sorbets are not the most popular flavors Four Seas offers, their popularity soars on extremely hot and humid days. Then, they are enjoyed as scoops or in drinks called "freezes" or "frosteds," frothy blended concoctions that combine sherbet or sorbet with soda water or lemon-lime soda.

KEEPING QUALITY ALIVE

A midsummer cone of mint chocolate chip drips down a customer's hand. The mint chip at Four Seas is pink because it is made with peppermint, not spearmint like most parlors. *Photo by Audra Bayette/ Roots Workshop.*

Like his father before him, Doug Warren tastes every single batch of ice cream he makes. "I usually eat between a pint and a quart of ice cream on freeze days," he said. "I don't usually eat very much of it on days that I'm not making ice cream, but I never get tired of it."

From the mid-1950s until around 2000, when Doug and Peggy Warren took over the business, Richard Warren's process of making ice cream was virtually the same as his son's is now. Early mornings were spent making sure the correct amount of ice cream was made—not too much so that the product lost some of its freshness but not so little that a flavor would ever run out, even on the busiest day. He also sampled every single flavor without exception, whether they were his favorites or not, Linda Warren said. "He was extremely proud of his product," she said. "It's the truth, he tasted every single batch. And he had no cholesterol problems. It was amazing."

That process appears to be working, Doug said. He averages making fifty freezes per day, four days a week, for a total of two thousand gallons of ice cream weekly during the peak summer season. On an average Saturday in the summer, at least 1,500 cones of ice cream are sold. "And that doesn't include the sundaes or anything else," he said. "That's just in cones."

Like the process by which it's made and the machines it's made in, Four Seas' ice cream hasn't changed much in the nearly eight decades since W. Wells Watson first started churning it out using a tiny freezer in an old blacksmith shop. One of the store's signature flavors, chip chocolate, was actually invented in that tiny freezer, Doug said:

> *Most people put in pre-formed chocolate chips, but our ice cream actually has flakes of real chocolate in it. The story goes that one day, Watson left some chocolate by the stove and it melted. He was curious of what would happen if he added it to the ice cream. And after adding it, he realized that it made a lot of different shapes and sizes of chocolate chunks. And everybody liked it because with every lick you're getting a little bit of chocolate mixed in.*

The chip chocolate ice cream—called that rather than "chocolate chip" because of the prominence of the chips in the frozen concoction— is still made the same way today. Chocolate is melted on one of four small burners on a stove near the ice cream making room. When it's fully melted and has cooled slightly, the liquid chocolate is added directly from its pot into the ice cream machine. When it hits the nearly frozen vanilla ice cream, the chocolate splinters into thousands of pieces of varied sizes. The same process is used to make peanut butter chip chocolate ice cream, which is peanut butter–based ice cream with those same splintered chocolate chips.

The chocolate used in chip chocolate and peanut butter chip chocolate was, like the 16 percent mix, deliberated on a long time before the Warren family decided what kind worked best, Doug said. He and his father tested different chocolates for their levels of creaminess, melting point, amount of cocoa and taste before settling on a bittersweet chocolate that comes in ten-pound blocks. "We try to get one that's not too sweet but not overly cocoa-y. I think it's a nice blend. And each chocolate you try has a different melting point, so you have to be careful. You don't want something that's too hard to chew on or something that's just going to melt the second you try to eat it," he said. "And as far as I know, this is the same brand we've used my entire life."

Dick Warren's trick, Linda Warren said, was to keep the chocolate in his basement through the winter to age it and bring out deeper flavors. "The older it was, the better it was," she said.

Another signature flavor that original owner Watson created was based on a sweet treat found across New England and still made in many kitchens. Called penuche (pronounced pen-oo-chee), the sugary sweet fudge is a popular alternative in the region to more well-known flavors of fudge. "You have peanut butter fudge, chocolate fudge and even maple fudge. But here in New England, we also have penuche," Doug Warren said. It was one of Watson's favorites, and in his early years as proprietor of Four Seas, he turned his favorite sweet into an ice cream flavor. To make penuche, candy makers mix a large amount of melted brown sugar with vanilla, butter and cream or evaporated milk and cook it until it reaches a consistency like traditional fudge. Often, cooks will add nuts, especially pecans or walnuts, before the mixture solidifies completely. To make penuche pecan ice cream, Watson adopted a similar method and melted several cups of brown sugar in a pot on the stove to add the characteristic caramelized flavor of penuche fudge. Like the chocolate for chip chocolate ice cream, the melted brown sugar is cooled somewhat, and in this case, a small amount of ice cream mix is added to turn it into a creamy mixture that is then poured into the ice cream.

"If you're not a true sweet tooth, it's probably not the best thing to get," Doug joked. But it was his father's absolute favorite flavor and one of his too, Doug said. It's also one of the flavors that fans of the store have come to associate with Four Seas.

But it's not the only flavor Four Seas fans consider among the store's "signature" tastes. That honor also lies with several of the fresh fruit flavors that are only made for a few weeks each summer. For a few short weeks each year, three flavors—fresh peach, fresh strawberry and fresh cantaloupe—are rotated into the regular flavor stock. "We're definitely known for the fruit flavors here. And that's probably because we use real fruit, unlike a lot of places that use fruit extracts. Extracts are easy. But we use real bananas, real peaches, real ginger," Doug said.

Fresh cantaloupe is the first of the three fresh fruit flavors to be made every season. Beginning in June, when cantaloupes begin to come into the local fruit market at their peak, Four Seas begins buying them by the case. But the fruit waits a few days more on the shelves until it's extremely ripe in order to get the best flavor from it. The cantaloupe is meticulously diced up by a Four Seas employee and then mixed with a small amount of sugar in a blender. The purée is added, as any other flavoring would be, to a batch of ice cream.

Peach is the next flavor to come along. Like penuche pecan, it has become synonymous with the Four Seas Ice Cream name, thanks to write-ups in many publications and famous fans such as several members of the Kennedy family. Around the Fourth of July weekend, peaches begin getting shipped from Georgia and the Carolinas across the country, including into New England and to the Centerville fruit market from which Four Seas has purchased produce for decades. The ice cream is made in the same manner as cantaloupe and also is made only for about two months. Though the store is now open during the winter months, making ice cream and selling quarts, pints and ice cream cakes, peach still isn't made year-round. Doug explains:

> *They grow peaches year-round in places like California, but the Georgia peaches are the sweetest, and the ones from North and South Carolina. They have great fruit, but the peaches aren't really tasty except in the summer season. We've never really enjoyed them during the winter months. They just don't have those flavors people look forward to all summer.*

Fresh strawberry ice cream is perhaps the sweetest treat at the store because it's only available for a period of about two weeks every summer. According to Doug, it's because of the short growing season for the local berries used in the ice cream.

> *The ice cream is made with local Cape Cod berries grown literally down the street from Four Seas. They're picked one day and made into ice cream the following day. We basically just chop them up, add a little sugar and we're done. And we sell it only as long as we make it. We try to make as much as we can during the two-week growing season, get as many boxes from our local growers as they'll sell us. And as soon as they stop producing strawberries, we stop making fresh strawberry ice cream and go back to using frozen strawberries.*

Customers who buy strawberry during that period are often surprised that the color of the ice cream is closer to a light pink than the nearly fluorescent strawberry ice cream that some other stores sell. It's because no additional flavorings or colorings are added so that the fresh, natural taste of the strawberries comes through. "Our regular strawberry is good, but it's just not the same," Doug said of his favorite flavor.

One fresh fruit flavor that Cape Codders looked forward to every summer isn't made anymore, Doug said—and though some customers might, he doesn't particularly miss it. Beach plum ice cream was made for many years thanks to the generosity of a friend of Richard Warren, a doctor who lived in the Cape Cod beach area of Sandy Neck. Beach plums are native to the area and grow like blueberries on bushes that grow heartily in the Cape's many sandy areas. As most residents of seaside New England know, beach plums might taste good, but turning them into jam, or in this case ice cream, isn't the easiest process. "Beach plums are about the size of a huge pearl, and inside of that is a seed. And to get those seeds out is just unbelievable," Linda Warren recalled.

Because he loved the flavor so much, Richard Warren's friend would do all the picking and pitting of the tiny beach plums and bring them in ready to be puréed and added to ice cream. Richard Warren would be able to turn the fruit into one single batch of ice cream—about twenty-four quarts and ten or eleven pints, plus three three-gallon tubs to scoop the ice cream. "This gentleman would get most of the quarts and most of the pints, so it was mostly a cone sale for one or two days, and everybody looked forward to it," Linda said.

But as the man aged and wasn't able to handle the bushels of fruit as he once did, the Warren family decided to take on the task themselves—and it didn't exactly become one of their favorites. "We did it for two years. But it was just so labor-intensive we couldn't keep it up. I don't have any idea how this gentleman did it," Linda said.

"We tried all kinds of different things to get the pit out of it," Doug said. "But when you've got a heavily pitted item, and this was with about 50 percent of the fruit made up of a pit, it's difficult. So that became the death of that flavor."

There are only a handful of ice cream flavors that have gone the way of the beach plum ice cream. In fact, images of a board advertising flavors at Four Seas in the 1950s show only a couple of changes: lemon sherbet has since been changed to lemon sorbet, and one of W. Wells Watson's signature flavors, spiced apple, is no longer made. But in an homage to that flavor, the store does offer spiced apple topping for sundaes. Another ice cream topping was also at one point its very own flavor, Georgia Thomas remembers. At one point in the early years of their ownership of Four Seas, Richard Warren created a crème de menthe ice cream. The strong green minty liqueur was

The board listing flavors at Four Seas, seen in the 1960s, features exactly the same flavors today—on the same exact board. *Courtesy of the Warren family.*

a separate flavor from the pink peppermint chocolate chip that is still made at the store. It was discontinued at some point but, like the spiced apple, is still a topping available for customers to choose in their sundaes. Doug Warren remembers that a flavor called honey macaroon was also made at some point but is no longer served. Richard Warren also came up with a few unique flavors that are no longer made, though his son did bring them back during a seventy-fifth-anniversary event in 2009. One was a popular old-fashioned flavor based on the Post brand cereal Grape-Nuts. The whole-grain cereal is a popular addition to ice cream in New England and some parts of Canada, and for several years, Richard made Grape-Nuts ice cream at Four Seas. Another Richard Warren original came about one year after the store had a surplus of chocolate chips and multiple kinds of nuts, both expensive ingredients that the cost-conscious Warren was loath to waste, Doug said. "He had a bunch of stuff left over at the end of the summer that wouldn't be good the next year. So he just dumped all the different nuts and chocolates into the ice cream maker with the mix as an easy way to use up leftover ingredients and called it 'trail mix' ice cream. And he said he actually got a good response, but it would have been an expensive flavor to keep making every year."

Even more flavors were never served, though they're in the Four Seas recipe repertoire. For decades, the recipes for all of Four Seas' favorite flavors have been housed in an old rusted recipe tin alongside other flavors that have been dreamed up by the store's owners but have never been served. W. Wells Watson, for example, included a recipe for tutti frutti ice cream. In high school, Doug Warren said, he experimented with several flavors that never made it to the ice cream counter for serving to customers. One of his favorites was a riff on the now-popular vanilla ice cream with chocolate sandwich cookies mixed in, usually called cookies and cream. But the experiment never had a happy ending, Doug said: despite freezing, the sandwich cookies could never hold up to the spinning blades of Four Seas' ice cream machine, resulting in pulverized cookies whose flavor didn't really come through. Two high school–era experiments of Doug's—amaretto ice cream and piña colada ice cream—actually made second appearances during the 2009 seventy-fifth-anniversary celebration alongside some of Richard Warren's old-fashioned favorites.

For other flavors, their elimination was due to waning popularity, in particular two flavors of yogurt that were introduced under Richard Warren but have since been eliminated from the flavor list. The frozen yogurts were introduced in the late 1980s after a nationwide desire for a healthier frozen treat led to yogurt shops cropping up across the country. As several chains sprung up and gained popularity, Richard decided to try his hand at the trend. "The only thing Richard ever put in that was totally against him, he really didn't want to do it, were the yogurts," Linda Warren said. So Four Seas began experimenting with different frozen yogurt mixes until a mix was found that was lower in fat but didn't sacrifice quality. Richard's first frozen yogurt flavor was orange pineapple, followed shortly by three other flavors: apple pie yogurt, red raspberry yogurt and blueberry yogurt.

The blueberry yogurt replaced a blueberry ice cream that the store had served, Doug said. The apple pie yogurt contained pieces of real fruit and pieces of piecrust. But by 2001, when Doug and Peggy Warren took over the store full time, frozen yogurts had fallen in popularity and were no longer being consumed at the rate customers had eaten them in the late 1980s and early 1990s. So the apple pie flavor, the least favorite of the four yogurt flavors, was discontinued. It was followed by red raspberry, which was similar in flavor to the black raspberry ice cream that is one of Four Seas' most popular flavors, Doug said.

Nationwide, yogurts have never reached the popularity of ice creams. According to the business publication *HighBeam Business*, in 2009, ice cream accounted for 61 percent of the frozen dessert market in the United States, or about 920 million pounds of ice cream. That same year, frozen yogurt was only 5 percent of the frozen dessert market, or just about seventy-four million pounds. It's a downward trend that Richard Warren expected all along, Linda Warren said. "At the time he added frozen yogurt to the menu, everybody was saying that it was the thing of the future, that it was going to replace ice cream. And he said, 'No, it's not.' All these yogurt shops were supposed to wipe out ice cream shops. But within ten years, they were gone. And ice cream is still here."

In 2011, one of the store's sorbets was also discontinued, not due to lack of popularity but because a key ingredient was discontinued. The manufacturer that Four Seas used for its raspberry purée discontinued the product. After several trials, no other companies or homemade products had a similar enough flavor that Doug Warren felt comfortable switching to them without customers noticing—and not in a good way. "We couldn't find the same raspberry flavor profile. And if we couldn't find one that tasted similar enough, then people were going to compare it to the old flavor and notice that it wasn't the same," he said.

So instead, the store moved away from a flavor it has made for decades into new sorbet territory. Over the course of the summer, four new flavors were introduced to customers, and feedback was taken about which were the most popular. The first flavor introduced was a take on a popular old-fashioned summer drink called a raspberry lime rickey. A mixture of soda water, fresh lime juice and muddled raspberries or raspberry-flavored syrup, the drink was enjoyed at soda shops across the New England region and is still made at some shops. Called raspberry limeade sorbet, the mixture of sweet-tart lime and purple raspberries became popular very quickly, Doug said. Next came another flavor that was a riff on a popular dessert the Warren family had always enjoyed: key lime pie. The key lime sorbet was initially too tart and crumbly, so coconut milk was added to keep it dairy-free but make the flavor creamier and easier to scoop into cones, he said. Next came watermelon sorbet, a popular option with children but one that didn't seem to appeal to adult customers quite as much. Pear and pineapple sorbets came next, and by the end of the summer of 2011, raspberry limeade and key lime sorbets proved to be the most popular. At least for now, they will be in the sorbet rotation along with the lemon sorbet that has been made for decades. But it isn't impossible that old-fashioned raspberry sorbet will be brought back at some point, Doug said. "It will be a while, though, so if we go back to it people hopefully won't remember exactly what the old one tasted like and we can try a new flavoring without problems."

Raspberry sorbet isn't the only flavor that has posed a challenge to the Warren family because a particular ingredient was discontinued. Over the years, some flavors have suffered because the old-fashioned nature of the treat just didn't bring enough money to manufacturers to keep producing the flavorings, according to Doug. But even basic flavors such as chocolate have changed slightly over the years because of the whims of flavoring manufacturers. Because of customers' expectations for the same ice cream they've eaten for decades, the Warren family has always gone to great lengths to try to keep the flavors as similar as possible, Linda said.

> *It was very important to Richard to keep things the same. He always kept on top of the ingredients. And if the manufacturer went out of business or stopped making something, he always got the recipe to see if another manufacturer would make it for him or if he could combine several other flavorings to come up with something similar. And in the winter after he found out the ingredient had been discontinued, he would test the flavors in his home ice cream maker. And if nothing would compare, he would begin making it himself.*

Another flavor that was subject to much experimenting and taste tests was ginger. For years, ginger ice cream at four Seas was made with a ginger product that contained real ginger and flavorings. But when that product was discontinued, Richard Warren went straight to the source. "Now we go to the farm stand and get real ginger and grind it up ourselves. It's a lot of work, but Richard tried to make sure his ice cream never changed."

SAME QUALITY, DIFFERENT FLAVORS

Doug Warren strives to keep things the same in flavors for which Four Seas is famous. But since taking over, he has expanded the number of Four Seas flavors for a number of reasons and to suit many different palates. Many of those flavors were created specifically for local restaurants—for example, a green tea ice cream for a local Thai restaurant and a vanilla and white chocolate ice cream for a snack shack near a harbor visited by tourists looking for ferry rides to nearby Nantucket and Martha's Vineyard. Other flavors were created for Four Seas' customers but are only available at certain times. At any given time, there are twenty-four flavors available for scooping at Four Seas. Those flavors that aren't being scooped at that time are available in pints and quarts to take home. For example, rum and butter ice cream and caramel crème ice cream are rotated together; when one is out at the fountain and not available for scooping, the other one rotates in. So in 2001, when the apple pie and red raspberry frozen yogurt flavors were eliminated, there was an opportunity to fill what had become an empty slot in the rotation, Doug said. He and Peggy's first idea: make a riff on the sweet, spicy tea called chai they had been enjoying that summer. Peggy had begun adding powdered vanilla-flavored chai tea mix to vanilla frappes, and the concoction quickly grew popular among employees. At the same time, Doug said, he had started buying a hot version of the tea at a local coffee shop and felt it would make a great transition into ice cream. "It was a great alternative to coffee. It sort of reminded me of a Christmas cookie, like a gingersnap or a snickerdoodle." The flavor, a vanilla-based ice cream with cinnamon, ginger, allspice, nutmeg and other warm tastes, was invented and is still served.

Doug's next experiment came when he wanted to create a peanut butter cup ice cream. But unlike other ice cream stores, he didn't want to add peanut butter cups to ice cream; he wanted to make every bite of the ice cream taste like one of his favorite candies. The ice cream was created in the same manner that Four Seas' famous chip chocolate is, by adding melted chocolate to ice cream. In this case, peanut butter sauce that is offered to customers as a sundae topping was added to the ice cream. Once that was mixed, the melted chocolate was added to create a combination of peanut butter and chip chocolate in every bite. Today, peanut butter chip chocolate is one of Doug's favorite flavors, he said. "Fresh strawberry is my number one favorite flavor, no question. Fresh peach comes next, then penuche and peanut butter chip chocolate. After that it gets kind of muddy."

In 2009, Doug had the opportunity to experiment more than had ever before been done at Four Seas during a seventy-fifth-anniversary celebration for the store that included a new flavor—and sometimes two—every single week. "We had an opportunity to kind of shake things up without anybody questioning why we did it. So we created at least one new flavor every week for the seventeen weeks we were open. Before the season, I came up with a list of over sixty possible flavors to try. And I knew we had to narrow it down, but there were so many I wanted to try that we decided to have some weeks with two flavors."

The flavors were a new world for some Four Seas patrons, many of whom were used to the old-fashioned list that had been served at the store for decades. Inspiration for the many flavors came from everywhere, Doug said. A tangerine grapefruit margarita sorbet, which featured real chunks of fruit and tequila, was inspired by a drink of the same name at a local restaurant. Two, Grape-Nut and trail mix, were inspired by his father's experiments with those two flavors decades earlier. A fourth, maple-bacon ice cream, was a whim, Doug explained. Maple syrup was combined with ice cream in the machine. Bacon was baked in the oven with a sprinkling of brown sugar to caramelize it. Then, the crumbled-up bacon was added to the ice cream. Though it shocked some customers, he said, others still ask for the flavor, which was actually made for two summers after. Doug explains why he wanted to experiment:

> *It kind of goes back to my crafty nature, I think. I love painting and drawing and doing things like that. I get inspired by things I see, things around me. It's like any artist or any person that's creative. They take what they see and turn it into something they like, put their own spin on it. A good cook will take a recipe and turn it around and make it taste better than the recipe their food was originally based on.*

One flavor that originated during the seventy-fifth-anniversary celebration holds a special place in the Warren family's heart. The flavor, called Craigville Beach, is an ode to the nearby beach that is a first stop for many families on a summer day—right before they visit Four Seas in the late afternoon during something employees call the "beach rush." "I wanted to have something with a local flair to it," Doug said. "So we literally turned Craigville Beach into an ice cream."

The inspiration came from what visitors might find on a visit to Craigville Beach: the sand they walk on, for example, and the rocks and seashells they and their children might collect in the course of a summer visit. Doug's first thought for sand was to use sugar to represent the gritty texture, but in order to add it to ice cream, it needed to be taken a step further. Here he took inspiration from a favorite customer from his time at Haven's Candies in Maine. The store sold many kinds of roasted nuts, but the most popular was a "burnt" peanut that was roasted longer than the others. One man, a priest, took the burnt flavor to another level, Doug said: he ordered wholesale-sized batches of the peanuts and asked that they be triple-roasted. "I think it's the closest to hell he probably ever got," he joked. "Plus, I knew burnt sugar was kind of a novelty item at the time, and I wanted to try it in ice cream."

The gritty sand took the form of sugar, caramelized on the stove in the same way brown sugar is burned for penuche pecan ice cream. When the liquid sugar hits the ice cream, it splinters and creates pieces of "sand" throughout the vanilla-based ice cream. Dark and white chocolates are also melted and added, still in their liquid form, to the ice cream. The liquid chocolate in Four Seas' chip chocolate and peanut butter chip chocolate flavors is cooled slightly so that flecks of chocolate in the ice cream are large. But in Craigville Beach ice cream, the dark and white chocolates are added in still molten form so that the flecks are tiny, Doug said. With the sand covered, the company moved on to adding rocks (macadamia nuts) and seashells (candy-coated chocolate pieces shaped like seashells made by a local candy company). "It almost seemed like every lick was a different taste," Doug said.

The seventy-fifth-anniversary celebration wasn't the end of experimentation for Doug. In the years since, he has spent time on top of his regular ice cream making working with new flavors. The next year, in 2010, to celebrate the grand reopening of a local Centerville liquor store, Four Seas created a chocolate red wine ice cream. That was followed up in 2011 with a red wine ice cream with chocolate chips in it to "really have the flavor of the wine come through," Doug said. "I just really enjoy looking at a flavor or a concept and asking, 'How can we really do that well?' And that's how we come up with flavors like the red wine ice cream."

In the winter of 2010, Four Seas began opening in the winter to sell pints and quarts, meaning that flavors people associated with the holidays now had a chance to shine among the more summery flavors. Flavors including pumpkin pie, eggnog and gingerbread with white chocolate chips were introduced and stocked during the holiday season. At that same time, ice cream cakes were also introduced to the lineup. And with ice cream cakes came an opportunity to experiment even further with ice cream flavors as riffs on popular cake combinations. While the most popular ice cream cake is a combination of chocolate and vanilla ice cream sandwiching hot fudge and crunchy cake pieces, Doug has also begun creating flavors specifically for ice cream cakes. For Valentine's Day 2012, two new flavors specifically for cakes made their way into holiday cakes. After seeing the popularity of red velvet cake with cream cheese icing rise in local restaurants and nationwide, it was time to try it as an ice cream cake, Doug said. The cake flavor, a combination of chocolate and vanilla with copious amounts of cream cheese icing, lent itself well to ice cream, he said. The cream cheese layer demanded more experimentation.

I nixed the idea of creating a three-layer ice cream cake with cream cheese frosting between the layers so I needed to create a cream cheese ice cream. I created a batch of ice cream with six blocks of cream cheese, or about forty-eight ounces of cream cheese. But I didn't think someone would want to just eat a lot of cream cheese–flavored ice cream, so I also added some traditional cheesecake flavors to it, too. It's pretty dense, rich ice cream, and that's what those red velvet cakes are supposed to be about: decadence.

Every winter, Doug continues to experiment with flavor combinations that previously only made it to the freezers of family members and friends. Others make it only into quarts and pints, not out front to the fountain area for scooping, he said:

You can't just kill off our other flavors. The only reason peanut butter chip chocolate and vanilla chai made it onto the regular flavor list is because we got rid of two yogurts. People get upset when they have to wait for their favorite flavors to rotate in, and adding more flavors to the list would mean they'd have to wait even longer. If we had the room and could add another chest and another twelve flavors, I would do it in a heartbeat. But since we have no more room, my flavors are sometimes made only once.

But there are other ways to ensure that customers' favorite flavors can be purchased, he said. On Cape Cod, which has a large Brazilian immigrant population, some of those flavors include tropical fruit ice creams that are sold in Brazilian supermarkets and restaurants. In 2010, a Brazilian friend of Doug Warren's suggested he expand his repertoire of tropical flavors to appeal to the population. Four Seas' coconut ice cream, one of its top sellers, was already popular, she told him—but an easy way to expand his popularity in the Brazilian community was to create even more flavors that reminded people of their favorite childhood flavors. In much the same way that many people's childhood flavors are incorporated into Four Seas' traditional flavors, Doug went about creating traditional Brazilian flavors with the quality of Four Seas' other flavors. Passion fruit was the first flavor made, with a natural passion fruit concentrate because "you're not going to get the real fruit here locally too often. But it went really well, so I kept on going down her list of suggestions." Next were guava, made with guava nectar, and pineapple. Doug experimented with both sorbets and ice creams, "and they liked it better creamy, so we started selling it at the local Brazilian market."

No matter what flavor Doug Warren comes up with, it's a good bet that a lot of trial and error went into it before it was sold to customers, either for scooping or in quarts and pints. It was a three-year process for Doug and Peggy to come up with a s'mores flavor they could be proud of, Doug said. They had always wanted to turn the campfire dessert favorite—two graham crackers with a piece of chocolate and a marshmallow melted in between—into an ice cream. "But it took us several years without even selling it. We made it multiple times as an experiment." The first attempt at s'mores ice cream, in 2008, was marshmallow-flavored ice cream with melted chocolate added in to create Four Seas' signature chocolate chunks. Regular graham crackers would get soggy, Doug reasoned, so he started at an unusual place: a cereal flavored like graham crackers. The pieces were covered in a sugar glaze. But the ice cream was still soggy, and a second problem cropped up. "When you tasted it, you could taste the chocolate and the marshmallow, but you couldn't really taste the graham cracker right away. It was sort of a secondary flavor. And I didn't like that. I wanted every single flavor to be there every time, like every lick tasted like a s'mores."

Next came a chocolate ice cream with marshmallows and real graham crackers, but the chocolate flavor was too strong and the graham crackers couldn't stand up to the ice cream machine's two churning blades. "We put them in whole, we refrigerated them, we froze them and they still got pulverized," Doug said. A final marshmallow-flavored s'mores ice cream with chips of chocolate and chocolate-covered graham crackers worked better, but it still wasn't exactly right. So in the winter of 2011, after the store closed for the summer, Doug went back to work on the s'mores concept—this time with the idea to combine the chocolate and graham cracker flavors in the ice cream and then add marshmallows. It came together with a natural graham cracker–flavored concentrate, Four Seas' basic chocolate ice cream recipe and the marshmallow cream used for sundaes. "This time, every bite you got had all three flavors," Doug said.

A flavor that has become a standard during the holiday season also required trial and error, though in this case, it all happened during the course of making one batch of ice cream. "We did a lot of research into how gingerbread is made and wanted it to taste exactly like a gingerbread cookie. We weren't trying to reinvent the wheel. You shouldn't have to be told it's gingerbread in order to know it's gingerbread," Peggy said. Throughout the making of the first batch of gingerbread ice cream, Doug and Peggy added fresh ginger and "the Christmas spices you're used to in gingerbread," she said. White chocolate chips were also added to provide a sweet balance to the spicier flavors already in the ice cream. But something was still missing, and right before the ice cream was completed, some molasses was added. The flavor has been made for two winters now and is sold during the holidays and provided as samples during the village of Centerville's annual Holiday Village Stroll, when residents gather for cocoa and camaraderie provided by local businesses and residents.

Keeping It Simple

Despite the experimentation that goes on in the ice cream room, there are a few things Four Seas customers won't see in their ice cream—namely, candy bars and cookies. Though Doug experimented with adding chocolate sandwich cookies to ice cream while he was in high school, that flavor never would have been allowed out front for scooping, he believes. Under Richard Warren, ice cream was sacred. Doug explains:

> *Number one, it was Chief's philosophy to "taste the ice cream, not the crap that goes into the ice cream." Those were always his words. He believed that it might be fun to have Milky Way bars or Snickers bars in your ice cream, and maybe really novel. But you're not tasting the ice cream. You could put candy bars into soft serve and make it taste good. But to stay true to being an old-fashioned ice cream shop, Chief had to keep signature flavors that were true to that mantra. The only one he succumbed to, the only true kids' candy-like flavor, is chocolate chip cookie dough.*

Four Seas' version of ice cream with candy in it, Doug said, is very different than many companies'. There are only a handful of flavors that

A Four Seas Ice Cream classic sundae. *Photo by the author.*

contain any sort of addition aside from molten chocolate added to create chunks in the ice cream. Butter crunch ice cream (a butterscotch ice cream with butterscotch candies) and peppermint stick ice cream (a traditional New England ice cream with red and green mint candies in pink peppermint ice cream) are the only two flavors that contain candies. Mint chocolate chip—which is pink, not green like at most ice cream shops—and mocha chip contain two different types of chocolate chips. And chocolate chip cookie dough, of course, contains pieces of dough. But beyond those flavors, it's unlikely that customers will ever see candy concoctions, Doug said. Some ice cream stores might instead offer candies and cookies as toppings, but that isn't likely to happen either, he said. In fact, newcomers visiting Four Seas for the first time are often surprised that even sprinkles—chocolate or multicolored—aren't offered. "We won't put wax on our ice cream, and that's what they're made of," Doug said.

In addition to Richard Warren's strict adherence to old-fashioned flavors, Four Seas will never use commercial continuous-freeze ice cream makers, meaning that candies and cookies will always have a problem making it past the spinning blades of Four Seas' batch freezer. Doug said:

> *It's difficult to do those flavors with our machine. It chews things up and spits them out into tiny little pieces. Most people with batch freezers add candy or cookies after they make the ice cream. They'll chop up ten or twenty cookies and stir them into the mix before it goes into the freezer. But with 30 percent of our business going out the door in quarts and pints, you can't just sit there and fill pints and quarts with cookies. We would have to charge two different prices, one for regular flavors and one for candy-filled ones, and we're not going to do that.*

A third reason add-ins will never be part of the Four Seas menu is that the Warren family firmly stands behind the quality of the ice cream. With fresh fruits and quality chocolates, the flavor of the ice cream itself is more than enough flavor, Doug said:

> *There are a lot of flavors out there that, personally, I wouldn't mind in the ice cream. But part of me is stuck, too, on keeping that old-fashioned flair. I mean, we'll never even have double-double chocolate. Your chocolate should taste like chocolate in the first place. You shouldn't have to have it explained to you that it's extra-chocolatey."*

The quality of the ice cream is what changed Peggy Warren's mind about ice cream in general, something she never ate before marrying Doug and moving to the East Coast to run Four Seas, she said:

> *Before Four Seas, ice cream didn't really have much flavor to me. It wasn't worth the calories. I was especially not a vanilla ice cream person unless it was covered in something. But I can tell you, I eat a cone of vanilla at Four Seas and I really enjoy it. You can close your eyes and still identify the flavor you're eating here. It's that good. If I want all that junk in your ice cream, I'll go freeze a Snickers bar.*

A four-legged fan of Four Seas Ice Cream. *Photo by Linda Crayton/Roots Workshop.*

The insistence on basic flavor combinations doesn't seem to faze Four Seas' biggest fans. In line with a national trend, vanilla is and always has been Four Seas' most popular flavor by far. "It's just used for a lot of things. It's in sundaes and banana splits, it's used to make black-and-white frappes. And if you're going to introduce something to a baby or give it to a dog, that's the flavor it's going to be," Doug said.

In one year, Four Seas makes an average of 200 batches of vanilla ice cream, at about ten gallons each. The store sells an average of 2,400 vanilla quarts, 740 vanilla pints and almost 500 vanilla cans—or the average of twenty-five thousand cones—every year. Only 139 batches of the next most popular flavor, chip chocolate, are made each year. That's followed by 131 batches of chocolate ice cream. The next most popular flavors are black raspberry and coconut ice cream, Doug said. "But without question, vanilla blows them all away."

Chapter 7

ACCOLADES FROM NEAR AND FAR

Since the very first radio spot about Four Seas Ice Cream aired on a Canadian radio station in the 1940s, the seventy-seven-year-old Centerville ice cream store has received accolades and attention from across the country. Celebrity sightings helped put the store on the map, but well-respected publications from across the region, as well as across the country, helped cement Four Seas as a favorite ice cream store for those traveling from a few miles away or a few hundred miles away.

Locally, Four Seas is synonymous with the sweet treat. Just a couple of months after the Canadian radio broadcast about Four Seas, a reporter at the local daily newspaper, the *Cape Cod Standard Times*, as it was known then, wrote a glowing article about the store. Coincidentally, the reporter had worked at Four Seas Ice Cream as a teen and was eager to share her experience. But since then, dozens of articles have been written about the store in the newspaper, now known as the *Cape Cod Times*, and other local magazines. For over a decade, Four Seas has been named the best ice cream by *Cape Cod Life* magazine. And further, Boston publications have been recognizing Four Seas as having some of the best ice cream in the region as well. The "Phantom Gourmet," an anonymous reviewer who makes the rounds in New England both in numerous books and on a weekly television show, called Four Seas "the Greatest" ice cream parlor on the Cape and had this to say about the store:

> *Four Seas is a darling soda shoppe with parlor chairs, swivel stools, old-fashioned dipping cabinets, and blue flower boxes outside. They have the*

One of the many paintings that have been done of Four Seas over the years. This one shows the tradition of neighborhood kids showing up as early as 6:00 a.m. on opening day to be the first ones in line to get free cones. *Courtesy of Joan Scudder.*

longest-running ice cream tradition on the Cape…made with an awesome sixteen percent butterfat content and very low overrun. They refuse to top their superior scoops with cheap jimmies, but who cares when you can load up on homemade sauces like butterscotch, blackberry brandy, or crème de menthe. Four Seas is even responsible for inventing several flavors like chip chocolate, penuche pecan, and cantaloupe.

In 2005, *Boston* magazine recognized Four Seas as the best ice cream in the region, naming several of its flavors their favorites and praising the store's help, too. "It doesn't get sweeter than Four Seas, where flavor favorites include lemon crisp and peach, and homemade toppings range from melba sauce to crème de menthe. Best of all: You can eat your treat knowing your tips are put toward college funds for employees, all of whom are required by the owner to maintain good grades."

But it hasn't been just local publications that have recognized Four Seas as one of the best ice cream stores in the country. In 1998, *USA Today* named Four Seas the seventh-best ice cream in the country. In the article, Rick

Sebak, an ice cream reviewer and producer of the PBS documentary *An Ice Cream Show*, which extensively featured the store, said Four Seas was "the best total experience of all [ice cream places] I've visited" and praised the lobster salad sandwich as "dynamite." And just a year later, in 1999, the Sunday *New York Times* wrote a full-length feature article on Four Seas and called its product "indisputably delicious."

In 2000, Fox News Channel featured Four Seas during a Fourth of July broadcast called "Celebrating Summer with Four Seas Ice Cream," where it took a tour of the store, chatted with customers and sampled a few flavors. "There's a sure-fire way to tell it's summer on Cape Cod: Four Seas Ice Cream is open for business," the broadcast stated.

In 2003, *People* magazine hosted a lighthearted tasting contest featuring sixteen handpicked favorite ice cream stores. Various flavors were reviewed by celebrated chef Rocco DiSpirito, food writers Jane and Michael Stern, Homer Simpson of the Fox cartoon show *The Simpsons*, *Spy Kids* stars Alexa Vega and Daryl Sabara and Penn State University Creamery head Tom Palchak. The panel rated Four Seas three "scoops" out of five.

Food-centric magazines have also taken notice of Four Seas' high-quality ingredients and scrupulous production. *Gourmet* magazine featured Four Seas as one of its favorite places in 1998, and *Food and Wine* magazine twice recognized Four Seas as one of the best ice cream producers in the United States. In 1983, *Food and Wine* praised Four Seas with these words:

> *Knowledgeable visitors to New England are apt to detour many miles to visit an irresistible attraction in tiny Centerville, Massachusetts, an unspoiled Cape Cod town just outside of Hyannis on Nantucket Sound. The Four Seas Ice Cream Store, located in what was the village smithy's shop, is owned and operated by a local high school guidance counselor, Dick Warren. From just before Memorial Day to just before Labor day, when Four Seas is open, Warren makes his superb ice creams in a single freezer in the back of the store. Although the rich and creamy vanilla is the best seller…sundaes of homemade hot fudge on coconut ice cream are another prime treat.*

Nearly thirty years later, in 2011, the prestigious magazine again praised Four Seas—including the coconut ice cream—in its list of the "Best Ice Cream Spots in the U.S."

In 1998, competitor *Gourmet* magazine also recognized Four Seas in a lengthy write-up by the Sterns, known food writers and authors of the "Roadfood" series and website:

Born Loser creator Art Sansom, a huge Four Seas Ice Cream fan, has written many comics about the store, including this one, 2011.

The sundaes are a delight: claret sauce on chocolate ice cream is our undoing. Frappes are expertly blended. And there is one non-ice-cream item we need to note, the perfectly proportioned lobster salad. But the pride of Four Seas are the cones: small (one generous globe); large (one extra-big conical scoop), or double (two globes); the last is the maximum amount of ice cream any ordinary-sized cone can bear. The cone, of course, is the perfect ice-cream delivery system, allowing folks to eat on the stroll without cumbersome utensils, and also obviating interference from sauce, nuts, cherries, or whipped cream. This is not to impugn fudge or marshmallow cream, it's just that Four Seas ice cream is worth savoring with no adornment. It's honest and pure, luxurious but not ridiculously rich. This is ice cream you want to eat every night, all summer long.

Travel + Leisure magazine echoed *Gourmet*'s choice of Four Seas as one of the best ice cream shops in America in a 2008 article that said it was "the place for Kennedy sightings."

TIMELINE

1934
Irving Wolff, whose family owns Ye Olde Cape Codder restaurant in Centerville, Massachusetts, decides to open an ice cream store in the quaint Cape Cod village. His friend, Boston insurance man William Wells Wilberforth Watson, agrees to financially back the parlor.

1936
Wolff approaches Watson with a $600 debt after running the Four Seas Dairy Bar for two years. Watson decides to come down to Cape Cod in the summers to try his hand at running the store, which becomes very successful under his management.

1938
Watson purchases the Four Seas property and business for $6,500. In the next two decades, Four Seas begins to establish itself as one of the most well-known ice cream stores in the region.

WORLD WAR II
During the war, though many foods were rationed, ice cream was deemed a necessity to keep American happiness from failing. So Four Seas stayed open, usually opening by noon and running out of ice cream by four o'clock.

1954
Georgia Swift, a high school sophomore, begins working at Four Seas behind the counter.

1956

Boston University student Richard Warren finds a job listing for a Four Seas Ice Cream managerial position and accepts the job.

1957

Georgia Swift and Richard Warren marry. That same year, they move full time to Cape Cod, where Richard begins teaching full time at Barnstable High School in Hyannis.

1958–63

The Warrens' three children are born: Janice in 1958, Randy in 1961 and current owner Douglas Warren in 1963. The children spend much of their early years in a playpen in the sandwich kitchen at Four Seas.

1959

Four Seas closes the breakfast portion of the store. In the same year, Georgia and Richard Warren begin discussing the purchase of Four Seas Ice Cream with its original owner, W. Wells Watson.

1960

The Warrens officially purchase Four Seas Ice Cream from Watson.

1960s

With the election of John F. Kennedy as president of the United States, the Kennedy family and their fairy-tale "Camelot" story become the focus of Americans' attention. With their notoriety comes fame for Four Seas, one of their favorite summertime stops during their time at their Hyannisport compound.

1980

Georgia and Richard Warren separate. The family considers it the end of early thoughts of expanding to a second store.

1982

Richard Warren and Linda Joyal meet on a New Hampshire golf course.

1983

Randy Warren, son of Richard Warren, dies at age twenty-two in a car accident during spring break in Florida. The Warren family names a scholarship fund for local high school students the Randall Mark Warren Scholarship Fund in his honor and dedicates one day per year to raising money for the fund.

1984

Richard Warren and Linda Joyal marry at the top of a ski slope in New Hampshire. Linda takes over bookkeeping for the store and continued the job until just a few years ago.

1987

Four Seas holds its first-ever employee alumni reunion on Cape Cod. Of 133 alumni invited to the event, 129 and their spouses attended. It was one of Richard Warren's favorite memories of Four Seas.

1988

After fifteen years as a teacher and fifteen more as a guidance counselor, Richard Warren retires from Barnstable High School.

1988

Doug Warren moves to Yarmouth, Maine, and then Bowdoinham, Maine, and soon after begins working at legendary Haven's Candies, where he learns how to make chocolates and other candies. Decades later, he uses this knowledge to create unique ice cream flavors for Four Seas.

1999

After running a restaurant in Las Vegas, Nevada, Doug Warren moves with Peggy Wysocki back to Centerville to begin taking over Four Seas Ice Cream. They marry that September on Craigville Beach, just a quarter-mile from Four Seas.

2006

Richard Warren publishes *The Complete Idiot's Guide to Homemade Ice Cream*, which features many Four Seas flavors adapted for home ice cream makers, including the signature penuche pecan and fresh peach flavors.

2008

In January, Richard Warren, age seventy-two, dies in a skiing accident at Attitash Mountain in New Hampshire.

2009

Four Seas celebrates its seventy-fifth anniversary with a summer-long schedule of events, including days for local and national celebrities to scoop, a We Scoop for Chief alumni night to raise money for the Randall Mark Warren Scholarship Fund, a Cape Cod Ice Cream Idol contest for a new Four Seas flavor and new flavors every week.

RECIPES

These recipes, adapted by Four Seas Ice Cream owner Richard Warren for his 2006 book *The Complete Idiot's Guide to Homemade Ice Cream*, closely resemble some of the signature flavors made at Four Seas. Though commercial amounts of ice cream at Four Seas are made with mixes that contain cream and sugar already, the mixtures below are as similar as possible to the ingredients used at Four Seas, just reduced in scope to match the capacity of most homemade ice cream makers.

Make sure you have all of your ingredients and equipment on hand before starting to make the following ice cream recipes. If your ice cream maker requires ice and rock salt, make sure to have the required amount of crushed ice, usually about ten to twelve pounds, and up to five cups of rock salt. Remember that you'll need to keep adding ice and rock salt as the ice melts.

Also, if you're using an ice cream maker that requires pre-freezing of the container, make sure to do that prior to getting ready to make ice cream. It usually requires about twelve hours in the freezer.

You also may want to use a blender or food processor to create the purées required in the fruit flavors and many of the more unique flavors, such as avocado or tomato. And remember: fresh fruit ice creams are much better with the ripest fruits you can find, preferably when they're in season.

SIMPLE VANILLA ICE CREAM

(makes 2 quarts)

5½ cups heavy cream
1¼ cups sugar
2 tsp. vanilla extract

Mix the heavy cream, sugar and vanilla extract together until well blended. Cool mixture to 40 degrees F in your refrigerator. Transfer cold mixture into your ice cream freezer and freeze according to manufacturer's directions.

THE KENNEDYS' FAVORITE FRESH PEACH ICE CREAM

(makes about 2 quarts)

2 tbsp. gelatin (2 oz.)
½ cup warm water
12 large, sweet, ripe peaches (to make 2 pints purée)
1½ cups table sugar
1 cup whole milk
2 cups heavy cream

Place gelatin in warm water and allow to sit until completely dissolved (about 10 to 15 minutes). Wash, pit and cut up peaches, but don't peel. In a blender, purée peaches, sugar, gelatin and milk until smooth. Combine puréed mixture with heavy cream and mix well. Cool mixture to 40 degrees F in your refrigerator. Transfer cold mixture to the ice cream freezer and follow your manufacturer's directions.

CANTALOUPE ICE CREAM

(makes about 2 quarts)

1 large very ripe cantaloupe (to make 1 to $1\frac{1}{2}$ pints purée)
2 egg yolks
$\frac{1}{2}$ cup table sugar
1 cup whole milk
3 cups whipping cream

Peel cantaloupe and purée in a blender. Beat egg yolks and sugar together until light and fluffy. In a double boiler over medium heat, combine egg mixture and milk. Cook until the mixture reaches 160 degrees F, or until the mixture coats the back of a spoon. Remove from heat, cover with plastic wrap and cool in the refrigerator. When mixture is cool, add cantaloupe and whipping cream to egg mixture and mix well. Cool mixture to 40 degrees F in the refrigerator. Transfer cold mixture to your ice cream freezer and follow manufacturer's directions.

COFFEE ICE CREAM

(makes 2 quarts)

3 tbsp. instant coffee
$1\frac{1}{2}$ cups table sugar
7 cups light cream
2 tsp. vanilla extract

In a heavy saucepan over low heat, dissolve instant coffee and sugar in 3 cups light cream (do not boil). When mixture is dissolved, remove from heat and let cool in the refrigerator. Add vanilla extract and remaining light cream to coffee mixture and mix well. Cool mixture to 40 degrees F in your refrigerator. Place cold mixture into the ice cream freezer and freeze according to manufacturer's directions.

Brown Sugar Pecan Ice Cream (Called Penuche Pecan at Four Seas)

(makes 2 quarts)

3 egg yolks
2 cups whole milk
2 tbsp. butter
2 cups light brown sugar
2 cups heavy whipping cream
2 cups light cream
1 tbsp. pure vanilla extract
1 cup chopped pecans (optional)

Beat egg yolks until light and fluffy. In the top of a double boiler over medium heat, combine egg yolks with one cup milk and cook until mixture reaches 160 degrees F and coats the back of a spoon. When cooked, remove from heat and place in an ice water bath. In a heavy saucepan, melt butter and brown sugar together. Continue to cook over medium heat for one minute. The brown sugar will begin to darken. Remove from heat and slowly pour in remaining milk. If needed, return mixture to heat to incorporate milk, but do not boil. Cool until mixture is just barely warm. In a mixing bowl, combine egg mixture with brown sugar mixture, whipping cream, light cream and vanilla extract. Mix well. Cool mixture to 40 degrees F in your refrigerator. Place cold mixture into the ice cream freezer and freeze according to manufacturer's directions. If using pecans, add them just before ice cream is ready to be removed from the ice cream freezer.

LEMON SORBET

(makes 2 quarts)

2 cups table sugar (or to taste)
1 cup water
10–15 lemons (or 4 cups fresh squeezed lemon juice)
3 tbsp. lemon zest

In a heavy saucepan, combine sugar and water. Heat and stir until sugar is dissolved. Remove from heat and cool to room temperature. In a mixing bowl, combine lemon juice, lemon zest and sugar water. Mix well. Cool mixture to 40 degrees F in your refrigerator. Place cold mixture into the ice cream freezer and freeze according to manufacturer's instructions for making sorbet.

HOT FUDGE SAUCE

(makes about 1½ cups)

2 oz. unsweetened baking chocolate
¼ cup unsalted butter
2 tbsp. unsweetened cocoa powder
¾ cup table sugar
½ cup whipping cream
1 tsp. vanilla extract

In a double boiler over low heat, melt unsweetened chocolate with butter, stirring occasionally. Keep in the double boiler. In a mixing bowl, mix together cocoa and sugar. Stir in whipping cream and mix well. Add cocoa/ sugar mixture to melted chocolate mixture. Cook over low heat until sugar and cocoa are dissolved. Remove from heat and cool slightly. After chocolate has cooled for about 5 minutes, stir in vanilla. Mixture can be served hot or refrigerated for later use.

BIBLIOGRAPHY

Begley Bloom, Laura. "The Best of Cape Cod." *Travel + Leisure*. Last modified July 2008. Accessed February 1, 2012. www.travelandleisure. com/articles/the-best-of-cape-cod.

Boston Herald. "The Clan's All Here." July 19, 1986.

Boston Magazine. "Best of Boston." July 2005.

Bryant, Gregory. "Off 28, an Old Village Awaits." *Cape Cod Times*, March 23, 1997.

Corneliussen, Amy. "Centerville Collector Scoops Up Ice Cream Items of All Flavors." *CapeWeek, Cape Cod Times*, July 5, 1991.

Emery Thompson. "First Batch Freezer." Accessed February 1, 2012. emerythompson.com/firstbatchfreezer.pdf.

Fox News. "Celebrating Summer with Four Seas Ice Cream." Last modified July 3, 2000. Accessed January 15, 2012.

Haskins, George. *Cape Cod Handbook*. Hyannis, MA, 1936.

Highbeam Business. "Ice Cream and Frozen Desserts Market Report." Last modified 2012. Accessed February 25, 2012. business.highbeam.com/ industry-reports/food/ice-cream-frozen-desserts.

Katz, Gregory, and Trick Darcy. "JFK Daughter Will Marry Longtime Beau." *USA Today*, July 18, 1986.

Kennedy, Edward M. *True Compass: A Memoir*. New York: Twelve Books, 2009.

O'Connell, James C. *Creating a Seaside Resort*. Hanover, MA: University Press of New England, 2003.

Orlando Sentinel. "Names and Faces." July 23, 1986.

Ouellette, Jen. "Getting the Scoop on an Ice Cream Legend." *Register.* Last modified July 9, 2008. Accessed March 25, 2012. www.wickedlocal.com/barnstable/news/x518434456/Getting-the-scoop-on-an-ice-cream-legend.

Pennsylvania State University. "Ice Cream Short Course: Learn the Ins and Outs of Ice Cream Manufacturing as Knowledgeable Instructors Take You from 'Cow to Cone' at the Annual Penn State Ice Cream Short Course." Last modified 2012. Accessed February 13, 2012. foodscience.psu.edu/workshops/ice-cream-short-course.

People. "Here's the Scoop! A PEOPLE Panel Gives America's Hometown Ice Creams the Sweet Test and Names the Very Best." September 8, 2003, 109–10.

Phantom Gourmet Guide to Boston's Best Restaurants. New York: St. Martin's Griffin, 2006.

Richards Miller, Ruth. *Centerville: The Seven Villages of Barnstable, Written by Its People on the Occasion of the 200th Birthday of the United States of America.* Edited by Town of Barnstable. Binghamton, NY: Vail-Ballou Press, Inc., 1976.

Rimer, Sara. "Prized Ice Cream Jobs Create Extended Family." *New York Times,* Sunday edition, July 25, 1999.

Sebak, Rick. "Great Places to Get the Scoop." *USA Today,* July 24, 1998.

Stern, Jane, and Michael Stern. "RoadFood." *Gourmet,* July 1999.

————. *Roadfood: The Coast-to-Coast Guide to 500 of the Best Barbecue Joints, Lobster Shacks, Ice Cream Parlors, Highway Diners, & Much More.* New York: Broadway Books, 2002.

University of Wisconsin. "University of Wisconsin Dairy Foods Short Courses." Accessed February 13, 2012. dairyfoods.wisc.edu.

Vida, Vera. "Bride Keeps Veil of Secrecy Over Wedding." *Patriot Ledger,* July 18, 1986.

Warren, Dick, and Bobbi Dempsey. *The Complete Idiot's Guide to Homemade Ice Cream.* New York: Penguin Group, 2006.

ACKNOWLEDGEMENTS

I would like to thank the entire Four Seas Ice Cream family for their memories, photographs and love of the little shop that has kept our family going for decades; the interviews and short conversations they had with me have added to this book and will always add to the legacy of Four Seas. I also supplemented their valuable firsthand knowledge with the extensive knowledge, support and photo library of David Still II and Edward Maroney at the *Barnstable Patriot* and Mary Sicchio at the W.B. Nickerson Cape Cod History Archives at Cape Cod Community College.

I would also like to thank Jeffrey Saraceno and The History Press for reaching out and seeing the special in our little roadside ice cream parlor. The sundaes are on the house the next time you visit.

None of this—the book or the history included in it—would have ever been possible without the fabulous Warren family, which for several decades has nurtured Four Seas into what it is today and for the past fifteen years nurtured my mother and me as if we were your own.

Chief and Linda and Georgia, you are the best grandparents anyone could have—and I say that for both myself and all the other employees who have felt your love over the years. Hail to the Chief!

Mom and Doug, thank you for giving me the opportunity to write this book, as well as your invaluable information. (And thank you, too, for forgiving me for the year I rebelled and worked at a rival ice cream shop.)

And finally, infinite love and thanks to Doug Number Two for the constant support, understanding and dog-wrangling while I completed this book.

Four Seas Ice Cream owners Douglas and Peggy Warren would like to dedicate this book to Chief. They would like to thank Linda, Georgia (also known as Mom and Grandma), Janice, Jennifer and all the friends, supporters and alumni who contributed to this book and who also contribute their time at the beginning and end of each season to keep the store going when its employees head back to school. You help us celebrate the history of Four Seas and keep it going for the next generations to enjoy.

ABOUT THE AUTHOR

Author Heather Wysocki spent her adolescent and teenage years behind the counter at Four Seas Ice Cream, the family-owned business run currently by her parents and her grandparents before that. She is an award-winning reporter for the *Cape Cod Times* and has written for several other Cape Cod publications. Wysocki is a graduate of Suffolk University in Boston and Cape Cod Community College in West Barnstable, Massachusetts. She lives in Marstons Mills, Massachusetts.

Visit us at
www.historypress.net